P9-CFZ-115

Independent Activities
for Creative Learning

Independent Activities
for Creative Learning
Second Edition

Helen Fisher Darrow

Theodore Lownik Library
Illinois Benedictine College
Lisle, IL 60532
WITHDRAWN

TEACHERS COLLEGE PRESS

Teachers College, Columbia University
New York and London

LB
1031
·D32
1986

Published by Teachers College Press, 1234 Amsterdam Avenue, New York, N.Y. 10027

Copyright © 1986 by Teachers College, Columbia University

All rights reserved. No part of this publication may be reproduced or transmitted in any form or by any means, electronic or mechanical, including photocopy, or any information storage and retrieval system, without permission from the publisher.

Library of Congress Cataloging-in-Publication Data

Darrow, Helen Fisher.

Independent activities for creative learning.

Bibliography: p.
Includes index.
1. Individualized instruction.   2. Independent study.
I. Title.
LB1031.D32   1986   371.3′943   86-1763

ISBN 0-8077-2805-5 (pbk.)

Manufactured in the United States of America

91   90   89   88   2   3   4   5   6

The function of intelligence is not to copy but to invent.

—J. H. Rush, "The Next 10,000 Years."
The Saturday Review,
January, 1958.

Contents

Preface

After seven printings, it seemed timely to revise the original edition of *Independent Activities for Creative Learning*. The first edition wore surprisingly well. Over a score of years, its repeated printings suggested that teachers were finding the book to be a useful, practical reference. It seemed to satisfy their need for ideas and procedures to help them branch off from daily, routinized programs of doing one workbook page after another, in one subject after another, as independent work. To accomplish this, the book offered over fifty examples of independent activities intended to stimulate students' growth as creative, intelligent learners. The activities were carefully designed to provide for creative thinking, along with practice in the "basics." They also were imbedded in a humanistic framework, suggesting worthy aims and appropriate planning techniques for classroom management. Means and ends came together in compatible partnership.

In these years of shifting sands in educational thought, with behaviorist theory for effective teaching and learning currently being emphasized, it seems more necessary than ever for teachers with a humanistic commitment and vision to hold firmly to an educational heritage that can be traced from Socrates through Rousseau, Dewey, Kilpatrick, and Piaget. This position holds that children should spend their school time developing their intelligence and creativity and that they develop most fully in an open, diverse environment that respects them as individuals, not as objects of lessons and test score numbers. In this position, effective teaching continues to be an art, not a pseudoscience. So with pleasure for having been invited to produce a second edition, and some regret that R. Van Allen, coauthor of the first edition, asked me to work alone this time, I present a new, expanded, updated edition, with more than twice as many examples of learning areas. The new edition speaks to a wider range of learner abilities—from disabled to gifted—and age groups—from primary through adolescence. It pays attention to Piagetian stages of development, from concrete through formal operations.

Special thanks go to Seattle teachers Ann Konertz and Beverly La Borde for their careful evaluation of the activity examples and suggestions. I hope the results of our efforts give teachers and children the lift they deserve: many joyous school days of creative, intellectual engagement.

Independent Activities
for Creative Learning

Chapter 1
Action for Independence

"I got a gooder idea than yours," comments a three year old to his partner in play.

With a firm "I can do it myself," a six year old refuses help with his writing.

"We work harder this way; it's not like the teacher telling you what to do and you're just doing it; we need to know how to take care of ourselves as we grow up," reasons a twelve year old in defending cooperative planning.

However expressed, there is common need among individuals of all ages to assert independence in thought and action—to be, in short, a *person*. Persons have the right to think, to speak, and to act for themselves. They have the inner resources to become self-directing. In a democratic society especially, persons have both the right and the responsibility to use these resources to make choices, the kinds of choices that become increasingly productive and satisfying.

INDEPENDENCE AS A LIFELONG VALUE

Growth toward independence as a person begins early in life and continues as encouraging experiences accumulate. Here, parents and teachers, the adults who most influence our young, hold a key position. By their actions, they choose to encourage independence or discourage it. By the degree of control and freedom that they provide, by the kinds of stimulations that they offer, these adults wield great power over the quality of experiences children will have. When children are given freedom to adventure and explore, inquire and express, discover and test for

1

themselves, all in an atmosphere of acceptance, they are being guided wisely. For them, the range of "adequate" responses has opened up and room has been made for recognition of their uniqueness. For them, acceptance has provided the necessary reassurance, support, and synergetic energy all humans need for taking the next steps in their growth toward independence.

Even with constructive guidance and encouragement, such growth is not always easy. Often pain and fear are involved in reaching out toward the unknown. Mistakes and failures are inevitable; there may even be occasional backward steps along the way. But if they meet success more often than failure, children learn to realize their worth as persons; the joy and pride in gaining confidence in their own particular strengths and talents makes the effort of reaching out worthwhile.

INDEPENDENCE IN THE CLASSROOM

When teachers recognize the value of encouraging independent thought and action, they make clear provisions for it during the school day. Individuals' need for time on their own will be given high priority, for it takes time to create—to search and originate, to organize and communicate newly formed ideas.

Also, individual needs for attention will be taken care of. As some individuals work independently, the teacher becomes free to work with other individuals or small groups who need help and guidance. This freeing of teacher time is an essential aspect of individualizing classroom work. Unless teachers find some time to work intensively with individuals and small groups, they are unlikely to deal effectively with the varying levels of abilities found in most classrooms. Without some provision for independent activities, the reality of individual differences can only be verbalized; it cannot be made operational.

The alternative to small-group instruction is whole-class teaching where everyone receives identical instruction, identical "assignments," and occasional individual assistance. Most teachers are aware of the futility of this kind of teaching, but they see no other way. Rightfully, they question the value of independent work if it means nothing more than "busy work" that fills time but has no substance. The question here is not whether children should have time during the school day to work on their own, but rather what shall transpire during that time. What activities can be profitably pursued in independent action?

SELECTION OF INDEPENDENT ACTIVITIES

The answer lies in determining those activities that are most likely to promote the dual goals of self-direction and fulfillment. Accomplishing this requires that carefully chosen criteria be set up to guide the selection process. Seven criteria are proposed here:

1. PRODUCTIVE THINKING

Will the independent activity require the use of productive thinking? Thinking put to use in solving problems and drawing constructive conclusions is known as *productive thinking*. Productive thinking results in ideas as well as products, in questions as well as answers and hunches. It seems to have no end. Individuals encouraged to function as productive thinkers learn that the present is tentative and that the future holds promise, for the best becomes something yet to be achieved: the best books yet to be written, the best paintings yet to be painted, the greatest discoveries yet to be made, and the greatest inventions yet to be conceived. Hence activities that generate *problem solving* are preferred activities for independent work.

2. FREEDOM OF EXPRESSION

Will the independent activity allow freedom of expression? When there is no one right response required from everyone, each has the right to express the world as personally perceived and organize knowledge in terms of individual impressions. It is this uniqueness of response that labels work products "mine" in a deeply personal sense and keeps them relevant and fresh, if perishable. Hence activities that reflect *spontaneity* are preferred activities for independent work.

3. USING INDIVIDUAL TALENTS AND SKILLS

Will the independent activity use individual talents and skills? When individuals are confronted with open-ended challenges, they are free to use a wide range of individual abilities. In classrooms where varied talents and skills are welcomed, everyone has opportunity to maintain confidence in being an independent worker. Each can take personal responsibility for searching through his or her own storehouse of accumulated experiences to find the appropriate skills and information to use in furthering independent study. Skills and talents in this sense become functional and practical. Hence activities that stimulate *individuality* are preferred activities for independent work.

4. CREATING NEW MEANINGS OUT OF OLD

Will the independent activity create new meanings out of old? As they work independently, individuals need opportunities to modify their thinking and add new learning to that already acquired. They need opportunities to take personal responsibility for bringing together in new, rearranged forms whatever they alone have explored. As they bring their material together, they will find new relationships between facts and ideas and new ways to arrange and order their materials; they will emerge with new insights and new ways of thinking. Hence activities that spark *intelligence* are preferred activities for independent work.

5. REACHING TOWARD THE UNKNOWN

Will the independent activity stretch the mind toward the unknown? Creativity often begins where "know-how" ends. In the story of human progress, those individuals who have made the most significant contributions to human development have been those who have not accepted conventional answers but have striven to discover alternatives. Creative imaginations lead us continually into new vistas of perception, thought, and innovations of all kinds. Hence activities that encourage *inquisitiveness* are preferred activities for independent work.

6. PRACTICING SELF-CONTROL

Will the independent activity provide practice in learning the kind of inner control that frees one to work productively? Wherever learners meet intellectual challenges, they face the need to control impulses and direct them into productive channels. They must be willing to overcome obstacles, persist through disappointment, and avoid distractions that interfere with the fulfillment of their plans. As individuals become fully absorbed and "lost" in their work, able to merge it into a spirit of play, they apply themselves fully to creative thought and production. Hence activities that call for *self-discipline* are preferred activities for independent work.

7. GAINING PERSONAL SATISFACTION

Will the independent activity result in personal satisfaction for the learner? "Inner Quest" is as much a factor in promoting satisfying achievement as "Intelligence Quotient." Wanting to achieve takes on as much importance as being able to achieve in terms of successful effort. Individuals who pursue self-determined goals and do so with wholehearted effort generally feel satisfied with what they have done. They have enjoyed their work and feel pleased with the results. This kind of success is self-renewing. It provides momentum to start again, to tackle new challenges with enthusiasm. Hence activities that lead to *pleasure* are preferred activities for independent work.

Obviously, some independent activities where individuals work on their own fail to meet the foregoing criteria and must be vigorously weeded out. Among them are coloring in outlines, tracing patterns or figures, computing predetermined answers, and copying stories from the chalkboard. Others include seatwork activities that require simplistic filling in, matching, or completing with predetermined "correct" answers. Such activities call for conforming, convergent thinking. While occasionally useful for testing purposes or special practice, they rarely stimulate originality and do nothing for individuality. To achieve creative learning, only those activities that call for open-ended, divergent responses and that meet the criteria for selection should be used.

INDEPENDENCE AND CREATIVITY

The criteria for independent activities show a close relationship between self-direction and creativity. For all we know, the creative act and the act of self-direction may be one and the same. Certainly they seem to form an integral pattern. As individuals *search, organize, originate,* and *communicate,* they create and express their individualities. They also direct their own learning, exercising both freedom and responsibility. In the process they come to realize and appreciate their personal strengths and wholeness as individuals.

When the dividends are so high, it behooves teachers to organize a program of independent activities that promises the most in promoting the goals of self-direction and fulfillment. The process of individuation is too precious to leave to chance.

Chapter 2
Organizing the Daily Program for Independent Activities

Whether children will experience creative thought and production in school life depends largely upon how the teacher has organized the classroom environment for creative work. The teacher has the prerogative, as well as the responsibility, to schedule blocks of time for creative expression and arrange classroom space for independent exploration.

The teacher also has control over which experiences students are allowed to use in creative work, which supplies and materials will be available, and whether or not to emphasize cooperative procedures in planning. To promote independent activities calls for open cooperative arrangements of management procedures. Although particulars will vary by teacher preferences and student abilities as well as by environmental limitations and restraints, in one way or another, certain general factors must be dealt with:

TIME

Teachers who keep their own classes throughout the school day, or work in teacher teams with full charge for planning the daily program, are best able to control their time. They can shift and adjust the times suitable for creative activities on particular days. Others must simply work within the time constraints they have. In any case, time plans might range from special work periods to staggered work periods for small groups and individuals.

Special Periods

Total class time can be blocked out for creative independent activities, daily or several times a week, either in the morning or afternoon.

With the classroom set up with material and spaces for working, the students choose to pursue individual interests or get involved in individual responsibilities within a common group interest.

Individual Interests

With individual interests, the choice of the creative independent activity is more or less left to the individual. How the period is organized varies, of course, with the maturity of the group and the teacher's own working style.

Ms. C, for example, keeps a sign-up chart on which her first graders sign their names according to their choices of activities listed on the chart: easel painting, chalk or finger painting, science table, block construction, arithmetic table, dramatizing story in TV, and others. Usually the signing up is handled by having someone read the chart. As each activity is named, a limited number of individuals volunteer for it and sign up then and there. (One year the teacher used clothespins with each child's name written on one. As children chose a particular activity, they clipped their pins on the "clothes-line" stretched across the chart.) After all have chosen, children move to their working areas. Ms. C helps some children to get started and confers with others as she circulates to give encouragement and help. Before clean-up, the group as a whole circulates to share results.

On certain days Ms. C introduces a new material or technique or plans a common experience for the group before the students explore further on their own. For example, one day near Christmas she discussed the use of three-dimensional techniques in using construction paper for making Christmas trees and ornaments. The group had planned to decorate their room. Individuals experimented with this method during independent time that day, making all kinds of original tree shapes and ornaments for display.

Ms. J, on the other hand, jots down third graders' free choices as the group thinks through possibilities suggested in a planning session the day before. This gives Ms. J time to get certain materials ready and the materials committee has time to get other materials in order. She keeps a record of choices in a notebook that has a group of pages set aside for each child. In this way she keeps track of individual and group choices over a period of time. She also jots down notations of accomplishments to give her a record not only of choices but of results. The record is used for individual conferences with pupils and as an aid for future planning to broaden the group's scope of activities.

Mr. P has yet another way of handling individual interests. He simply announces to his sixth graders when free time will be scheduled for the entire class, or children request the time. In addition to choosing an activity to do, students also choose whether to work alone or with others. Materials are located in centers of ongoing interests, such as science, social studies and literature, or in general supply areas around the room.

Early in the year the group charts a list of "Things to Do Independently and Materials Needed." Additions and deletions are made from time to time. Children refer to the chart whenever they wish but are not confined to the suggestions. During the free period, Mr. P helps individuals having difficulty of one kind or another.

Ms. S, in charge of a group of young primary children, simply arranges materials each day on worktables and floor areas. Children "go to work" upon arrival, deciding on their own which table or floor area to work at and what activity to choose to do with the materials available. The teacher circulates and gives suggestions or observes closely. The children decide how long to stay at a work area and what to create with the materials. (Buttons in a box, for example, may be chosen for a design arrangement, for counting, or for color study, as the child chooses.)

There are still other ways to accommodate individual interests in terms of time arrangements. Older children might simply write their activity choices in time blocks on schedule sheets:

9:00–9:30	Spelling and Vocabulary Practice
9:30–10:00	Space Study Group
10:00–10:30	Math Center Work
10:30–11:00	Reading
11:00–11:30	Illustrating and Writing a Book

Younger ones might use a planning sheet that allows them to picture-read some possibilities and put x's in the boxes of their choice. They can use the spaces for copying a title, certain words, or dictating a thought to the teacher at a later time when sharing accomplishments. The teacher might also use the spaces to write something special to the child. Figure 2.1 gives an example:

In some cases the teacher may provide individual planning charts or sheets which are quite specific and encompass a week or more. (See Figure 2.2.)

Common Interests

In these periods everyone works on a common group interest but in individual ways. Individuals still choose their particular activity but within the range of ongoing group project needs. In Ms. F's room, for example, the fourth graders decided to build an African scene for dramatic play in connection with their social studies interest in Africa's

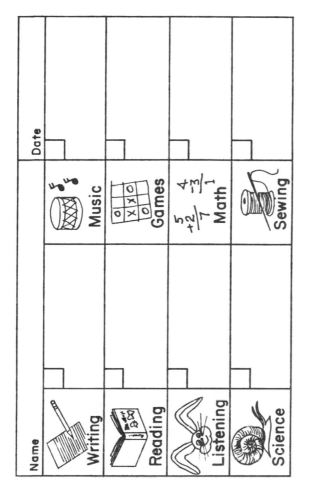

FIGURE 2.1: Planning Schedule for Younger Children.

FIGURE 2.2: Student's Individual Planning Chart.

Name: _____

ACTIVITY	DATE COMPLETED
Spelling	Mon. Tues. Wed. Thurs. Fri.

Spelling
1. Spelling book pages
2. Practice spelling words with flash cards
3. Give/take a spelling test
4. Make a crossword puzzle using spelling words
5. Practice penmanship using spelling words

Writing
1. Write to friends, relatives, or pen pals
2. Write in your journal
3. Write a story

growth and change. Ms. F listed items on the chalkboard as the group planned the scene. She then asked children to select items of interest to them and form committees to take responsibility for constructing them. Individuals hammered, sawed, painted, designed, scaled, molded, sketched, read, studied, observed, discussed, created, and evaluated as they contributed to the group's interest. Ms. F worked and conferred with the various committees as they continued their work.

Expanding Interests

Possibilities for choices grow and shift as new class concerns and interests arise, as individuals share personal experiences or ideas, and as the teacher introduces new materials and techniques for creative independent activities. Ms. B starts the year with only a few choices of activities—easel painting, drawing, writing, reading. As the children become accustomed to handling an activity on their own, she introduces a new one. By the end of the year the children engage in a wide variety of independent creative productions, including clay work, movie making, science experimentation, and wood construction.

Ms. K and Ms. L, team teaching with a group of older children, are careful to announce new opportunities for work each day or week, such as a special drama workshop, a history club, perhaps a visit with an international authority. They do this by posting a sheet with the titles and times scheduled and inviting individuals to sign up. On the other hand, the team of Mr. W and Ms. R prefer to introduce a new possibility each week by leading their group into a new study theme; a new art technique or material; a field trip to a nearby park, hill, or river to observe seasonal changes; a new poetry form; a new book, and so forth. They hope, thereby, to whet curiosities and stimulate new adventures and new ideas for creative, independent activities.

Expanding interests cannot be left to chance but should be deliberately planned as part of the program of creative independent activities.

Staggered Periods

When large blocks of time are scheduled for content study and skills practice, many kinds of flexible arrangements can be made for individuals and groups to use in working on creative independent activities at different times of the day. In this way creative thinking and producing penetrates the entire daily program as an integral part of the school day.

Small Ability Groups

Frequently small ability groups, composed of children functioning at a common level of skill achievement, should have the opportunity to choose creative independent activities as "seatwork assignment," in this way integrating practice with application.

In the small group, individuals may decide on a creative independent activity or select from various possibilities which the teacher provides. Here, too, time is required for establishing routines and practice habits of self-direction. Ms. F works with one reading group while two other groups work at their seats. At the beginning of the year she directs the follow-up activities, giving the capable readers, for example, experience in rewriting a story into play form; practicing oral reading for dramatization; making up original stories using the story characters; and composing comprehension questions on the story, involving why, where, who, how, and what.

As individuals become exposed to an assortment of activities and show ease in handling them, she shifts to giving activity choices by asking, "Do you have any suggestions for following through on this story?" Sometimes the class decides as a group upon one activity — writing stories or painting and writing. Sometimes individuals choose to work alone or with partners.

On certain days Ms. F uses practice sheets or certain paper-and-pencil tests for checking papers; other days she plans new experiences for the reading group. But most days are reserved for individuals to deepen their particular talents and follow their personal interests.

Ms. C often asks every member of a small reading group to handle a common responsibility but encourages individual expression. After reading a story of a family picnic one day, for example, everyone agreed to write and paint about similar personal experiences with family gatherings. The reading of a circus experience, likewise, was followed by each person choosing a way to express a personal circus experience, using paint, clay, paper, music, rhythm pattern, or words. In Mr. P's room a group of topnotch spellers, in lieu of spelling seatwork, prepared a book of word origins, hunting for strange and interesting words and determining their significance to people.

Small Friendship Groups

Small groups may be formed, not on the basis of ability in some skill, but by friendships. Friends with common interests work well together in choosing creative independent activities. Two, three, five, or six friends may cooperate in a thinking-producing endeavor. In Mr. G's fifth grade, self-selected committees took responsibility for preparing Thanksgiving stories for dramatic presentations. Individuals in each group accepted a special assignment: painting, making cardboard props, writing down narrative, designing costumes. At another time a small group of friends, becoming fascinated with poetry, decided to make an original poetry book. Various individuals took responsibility for making the covers, preparing the pages and book format, composing and illustrating poems, and editing the materials.

Invitational Groups

When the teacher offers choices, some of them might involve special skills that need guided instruction or, at least, a special introduction. Invitational groups generally should be composed of individuals invited to join for a clearly stated purpose. Ms. R, for example, says, "I'd like to have a poetry reading session where we'll read poems aloud and maybe look at different kinds of poems," or "I need to explain how a new math puzzle works. Who would be willing to work with me on it?" Of course, there's also room for a quiet request to an individual with whom the teacher especially wants to work.

Interest Groups

Interest groups are similar to invitational groups but are led by the children themselves, not the teacher. These may cut across both friendship and ability lines, bringing together individuals who might not otherwise have a basis for working together. A common concern for developing a campaign, a common interest in insect collections, and a common focus for a peace mural all may be reasons for individuals getting together in a cooperative venture.

Total-Group Projects

There are times, too, when the entire class becomes involved in a common undertaking, with everyone making a unique contribution to the group goal. During these times, while individuals are involved with their creative tasks, the teacher works with small groups on a variety of learning needs.

The subject of the skills practice or small-group learning experience need not be related to the subject matter of the ongoing project. Certain individuals may require special practice in an arithmetic process, in dictionary usage, or in spelling. Others may be ready for a new concept in arithmetic or a special study of word origins. A social studies or science-centered committee may need help in using the encyclopedia for note taking or in learning to find information by scanning. A committee may benefit from guidance in planning its presentation or verifying its information before reporting to the class. A science committee may wish help in setting up an experiment.

As way of illustration, Ms. C's first grade planned a bulletin board on spring clothes and textiles in relation to their study, entitled "Clothes: Sensibility and Fashions." Individuals made their own decisions regarding clothing designs to contribute to the project. As children designed, colored, and cut out their creations, the teacher selected a small group to bring to the chalkboard for practice in beginning consonant sounds. These children seemed ready to use phonics to help them attack unknown words. After a short session of work with the teacher, the children returned to their seats to resume their individual project work. Ms. C then called up another group of children, this time to count the milk and lunch money. These were children able to handle mental arithmetic beyond the processes taught in their grade. In the same way she helped another group to prepare a story for oral reading to the total class during snack time.

When the entire class in Mr. P's room planned to prepare an arithmetic book for display on parents' night, individuals chose to work on different sections and pages as planned by the group—history of arithmetic, uses of arithmetic, what arithmetic means, the number system, and so on. There were certain pages for which everyone had some responsibility, such as the page on "How to Make a Gallon." Each child illustrated one way to get a gallon of liquid, using small and large measures. Likewise, for the next page, "Gallon-wise," each child was responsible for drawing something that people purchase by the gallon. As individuals worked through their responsibilities in the arithmetic book, Mr. P used the time for small-group instruction and guidance. Over the days, he gave special help to certain groups of children, including those who had not yet mastered their fundamental arithmetic facts, those who had become curious about how slide rules are used, those needing help in hyphenating words by syllables when writing stories, those ready to explore new word meanings in their independent reading, those trying to write a play using correct play form, and those interested in finding out about rocket propulsion.

Rotational Groups

Class time can be arranged so that small groups rotate among a variety of independent activities or between required work and individual interests. To accomplish this, Ms. J assigned her second graders into groups at random, except for making sure that each group had leadership and some harmony among its members. Each group then spent time at one of five or six areas set up around the room, each area including five or six independent activity choices. Groups rotated so everyone spent time each day in every area.

Units of Work

Class studies and units of work present opportunities for some individuals and committees to be conducting research related to a study while others are pursuing different creative tasks also related to the study at hand. The teacher in these instances usually works intensively with one of the committees or small groups. In Ms. T's second grade, the class had become interested in the work of scientists and engineers, partly because many of the children's fathers were employed in such occupations. On a certain day while Ms. T worked with one group to help them read a story of scientists at work, others worked independently to record results of previous interviews with some of the fathers, or write stories and paint pictures related to the study at hand.

In self-contained and in team-teaching classroom settings as well, small-group, teacher-led instruction can easily be dovetailed with other group and independent activities involving all kinds of subject matter.

Individual Free Time

Many times individuals who complete required tasks quickly and need extra stimulation, or who are frustrated with standard curriculum for one reason or another, will make remarkable shifts in their attitudes when presented with time to pursue independent activities. Generally they respond well and need only space where they can work, sensible choices they can make, and materials on hand. Activity card files, wall-chart suggestions, group discussions, and individual conferences all help in guiding children who need a delineation of possibilities.

Routines and Responsibilities

Periods of creative activity require carefully set up routines and responsibilities. Once individuals learn how to handle themselves during such periods and agree to meet certain basic expectations for working on their own, they can be responsible for getting the most out of the time available for working.

Sometimes rules and standards can be discussed by the group in advance, with a small committee or the teacher taking responsibility for charting the rules for future reference. Frequently rules emerge in evaluation sessions from the problems arising during free-time activities. Children in Ms. C's room went over the routines carefully at the beginning of the year, each day practicing until they felt comfortable in handling themselves independently. In Mr. P's class, when a few children kept annoying others, individuals protested in rough arguments. During the evaluation period, Mr. P encouraged everyone who wished to speak on the problem. Together the group agreed upon a plan of mutual help: Everyone would try to anticipate difficulty by being alert to individuals who needed reminders of appropriate behavior or who might be invited to join up with an ongoing project. Individuals who felt especially restless or listless would try to recognize their feelings and ask for help. Thus the rule, "Help others and yourself to concentrate," was added to the chart of rules.

In a second grade, when confusion occurred around the paint area, Ms. B called for a discussion of the trouble. The problem seemed to be where to leave wet and unfinished paintings. Ms. B suggested that she might string a rope across the room on which paintings could be hung up to dry. Children agreed to contribute clothespins and chose a committee to take down dry paintings.

Ms. S insisted only upon individuals returning unused materials to their proper boxes and cleaning their table or floor spaces before leaving to take on a new activity. She concentrated on this kind of individual responsibility and courtesy to one another rather than building up long "rules" lists that so easily become confusing, irrelevant, and meaningless.

SPACE

Having a comfortable place to work is important for concentrated efforts at creativity. Individuals need space for themselves and space to express their ideas. Sometimes they use materials that require a larger working space than their regular classroom desk permits. When there is painting to be done, science experiments to be tested, or a puppet show to rehearse, the best place for working may be a corner of the floor, the back area of the room, a large table, the sink area, or outdoors. When there is deep thinking to do, a small corner separated from the rest of the room, whether by a screen or simply by two bookcases set at right angles, means a haven for the creative spirit seeking a sense of privacy.

Self-Service Areas

Students serve themselves in self-service areas or interest centers. Materials and ideas for independent activities can be arranged in simple fashion here and there around the room—on bookshelves, windowsills, small tables, or extra desks. Simple labels identify the areas, and various signs welcome the independent learner with suggestions such as

Come write.
Can you measure these?
What can you find out?
Watch our plants grow.
Paint a picture.
Be an artist.
Use these scientific instruments for discovery.

If tables and chairs crowd the interest area and there is no working space, children can use floor space in the room, in the corridor, or outdoors, or take materials to their own desks to use.

Self-service areas usually reflect changing class interests and concerns. Some teachers prefer maintaining a wide variety of fairly permanent areas from the beginning. Others set up only a few areas, simply changing the materials from time to time. As study and interests change, the areas change. Certain teachers like to start with a few areas and add new centers over the years so that everyone becomes familiar with a variety of self-service areas.

Ms. L keeps only a science area, a reading area, and an art center in her second grade. When children show a degree of satiation with the challenges there, she changes the materials. She places a fresh collection of books and pictures in the library area, discussing the materials with the group. If the science area has emphasized magnifying glasses and microscopic study of small animals and plants, she changes the focus to machine pulleys and levers for experiments. After clay has been introduced as a group activity, she adds a crock of clay to the art table, and so forth.

Ms. C also starts with a few areas, but over the months adds others: an arithmetic discovery table, a writing center, a museum of collectors' items. Whatever the plan for arrangement of self-service areas, routines and standards for their use need to be developed.

Study Centers

Teachers, working with the group, may set up all kinds of study centers, learning centers, stations, or areas for independent activities, sometimes related to a study theme topic, sometimes not; sometimes involving a whole class, sometimes just a small group or individual. Some are short lived, while others persist for longer periods of time. The focus of a study center may be one of the following:

activity (running a TV station, writing, telephoning)
topic (volcanoes, fables, good foods, famous people)
general subject (science, health, history, music)
specific subject (terrarium, vegetable or fruit collection, a caged bird, "Snoopy says")
drama (fantasy land, family life, hospitals, court room)
production (cooking, paper-flower making, a mural, a film)
skills (reading, handwriting, word study)

These centers can be housed in corners, in learning resource rooms, in a library and media center, in corridors and hallways, on radiator tops or counters, on tables, on walls, or in almost any open space so long as there is some definition to it, a designation that "Here is where we choose to work, study, and produce, alone and with others."

Managing Space

Individuals who know clearly where to go for materials and where to work when engaged in a certain activity can use initiative in handling the spaces available. Some teachers simply explain procedures; others choose to involve the group in planning space management.

Ms. A has her fifth graders help plan the space arrangement. She deliberately has the room looking bare when school begins in the fall. Then she presents the room environment as one of the group's first common problems. Together they decide where certain areas of interest should be, how to arrange the furniture, what needs painting, what the color schemes should be, and what the bulletin boards should be used for.

Committees take charge of the various self-service areas and bulletin-board spaces. The entire group sets up procedures for managing the space available. In this way students learn precisely what various spaces are to be used for, where to find materials, and which spaces are off limits for independent work, permanently or during certain times of the day. When group members become involved like this in planning their work space, they have the opportunity to practice and learn for themselves the skills of effective management.

Furniture Arrangement

In addition to variations in basic room arrangements, all kinds of flexible furniture arrangements are possible. When desks are movable and the room has tables, round and square, the furniture can easily be changed around from time to time for different activities.

In Ms. R's sixth grade, when students need to concentrate in a test situation or on individual research, they move their desks around the room for a comfortable place to work undisturbed. When committees meet to discuss, share, or work together, they arrange their desks in a square. For debates and total-group planning and discussions, children connect desks in a large open or closed circle. Having become accustomed to shifting their desks for different purposes of activities, children move the furniture with a minimum of confusion and loss of time.

Although desks cannot be shifted in rooms with screwed-down furniture, space for independent work activities can still be found. Floor space, corners, the outdoors, corridors, alcoves, windowsills, cloakrooms, tables, wall space, blackboard areas, bulletin-board centers, unused desks, old foot lockers, and drawer space—all serve as areas that attract the budding creator.

In team-teaching situations, one room often functions as a central workroom, where individuals and groups work on their own. Another room remains as a teacher-centered room where teacher instruction in small and large groups takes place.

Psychological Atmosphere

Sometimes classrooms are physically too small for many individuals to circulate freely. Sometimes classrooms are windowless or without sinks. These handicaps, of course, create space problems and limit the flexibility of movement available to meet childrens' needs. Teachers and classes then adapt as best they can, working within whatever limitations they cannot change. These limitations are external.

More important is the teacher's attitude toward the use of space for creative work. This is what we call the psychological atmosphere of a classroom. When individuals feel free to move around to find the "right" space for the work they have in mind, when they have been helped to learn how to move about for efficient use of time without disturbing others at work, the classroom gains a new space dimension—that of psychological support. It is this kind of space that encourages learners to reach out into the unknown with confidence and faith in their own abilities; it is the kind of space they need for growing as creative persons.

EXPERIENCES AS IDEA SOURCES

Ideas for creative independent activities emerge from reflection upon individual experiences that occur daily both out of school and in school.

Out-of-School Experiences

Because children are continually gaining all kinds of experiences out of school, planned or unplanned, the teacher who keeps alert to what they are can promote their use in school-related independent activities. The list could be endless:

Meeting relatives at airports, railroad stations, docks
Watching television and movie travelogues, documentaries, life stories, news reports
Traveling with family to mountains, beach, desert, other cities
Visiting grandparents, aunts and uncles, cousins, friends
Observing other family groups and home situations
Visiting hospitals, religious institutions, community centers
Talking with parents, friends
Taking trips to grocery store or to garage for car repairs, gas, oil
Going to the Post Office, United Parcel Service, Western Union
Listening to telephone conversations, family arguments
Hearing stories; reading books and magazines
Observing construction of buildings, roads
Observing clerking, servicing, policing
Attending picnics; visiting museums and art galleries
Playing with friends

Some families, of course, offer richer and more varied experiences to their children than do others. Children of stimulating families are easily at an advantage for idea sources, but even here, children may be rushed through one experience after another, with no opportunity for reflection and meditation so necessary for assimilation of experience.

Children need time to reflect upon and to reorganize the meaning of their experiences. "Reliving" their ongoing experiences by "playing" them through in fantasy and thought, allows children to reorganize, in Piagetian terms, their experiences into new constructs and equilibrations. In this way new knowledge grows out of the old. "Doing nothing" may actually be accomplishing a great deal in getting one's thoughts together for a leap into creative production. The school program undoubtedly should include time for this kind of open-ended thinking about experiences.

Teachers who understand the many individuals in the group will know which children are using time to think productively and which ones need help in doing so. They will be able to sense the difference between the kind of thinking-through experiences that result in creative activity and the kind of mind-wandering that leads away from it. Thus they can freely ask, "What are you thinking about?" and receive honest answers. In return, they will be able to learn to understand children's thoughts as well as their actions.

In-School Experiences

Because of the uneven, partial, and individual nature of out-of-school experiences, the school must continue to build firsthand experiences which children can use as idea sources. These experiences should be planned carefully to fill gaps in children's knowledge, to open new vistas of understanding, and to deepen understanding already achieved.

Firsthand experiences generally are more deeply absorbed than vicarious experiences and hence are more readily available as reliable sources of ideas for creative production. What children do, touch, respond to, and discover for themselves takes root as emotionalized learning. This is the kind that lasts. Vicarious experiences such as reading, talking, writing, and listening to other people's experiences also produces learning which, although it cannot replace firsthand experiences, can enrich thinking and even stimulate the reordering of firsthand experiences to new levels of awareness.

When children take planned trips, observe realities of life, handle real objects, plants, or animals, and test their feelings in action under teacher guidance, they gather up ideas that become rich sources for creative thinking and productive learning. This is what schooling is all about—to help children relive, rethink, and recall their many experiences, reconstructing them into increasingly higher-level, more clearly organized ideas and understanding. When children have the opportunity to talk over their experiences, listen to each other's interpretations, ask questions, and test their own answers, they get practice in becoming thinkers. They gain new ideas and deepen their insights. Their ideas get sharper, clearer and fuller.

Such situations should not be accidental but planned for deliberately, to stimulate new ideas and refine old ones so that children learn to think and feel more deeply.

Planned Common Group Experiences

Group experiences like listening to a story, visiting a community industry, interviewing an expert, viewing a film, handling an object, discussing a topic, or learning new words often lead to creative activities that go on for several days.

One rainy day Mr. T read rainy-day poems to his fourth-grade group. Later, throughout the week, individuals and small groups chose to work with the theme of rain: painting rain scenes and rain-inspired abstracts, preparing dramatic presentations of several of the poems, experimenting with the rain cycle, making cloth water-repellent, writing original rain poems, and the like.

After viewing a safety film, Ms. G's third graders constructed individual books of safety rules with original slogans and illustrations, kept records of observations of safety events, or wrote to ask the city safety inspector for an interview.

Planned Class Studies and Units of Work

A core study or unit of work involving science, social studies, literature, and other subject areas also can lead to creative activities. When children help to choose and plan the study, there is much opportunity for creative thinking and shared responsibility.

Ms. E's fifth graders showed curiosity about the new building going up as an addition to their school. As a result of the teacher's interest in following through with study, and further class discussion, individuals or small groups engaged in a variety of independent creative activities related to the study:

A cardboard model of the school site and buildings was prepared.
A mural of the history of American schools was painted.
A dramatic play of old and new ways of teaching was planned.
Information on public schools in America and in other countries was researched.

The meaning of school functions and workers was discussed.

The importance of community support was discussed.

A leaflet, "What Schools Mean," was prepared for circulation in the community.

In Ms. R's room some individuals volunteered to build a weather station in relation to the unit on weather and weather instruments on which the total class was working at the time.

Ms. T thought her group of second graders might be interested in an organized study of literature. As the group studied fables, folk tales, modern stories, and the like, there was opportunity for children, on their own or with friends, to write original tales, paint interpretations of stories, dramatize scenes in creative play, discuss their feelings about the stories, and construct puppets and stages.

Sharing Periods

Sharing personal experiences and learning during talk periods is another way for children to build idea sources for creative expression. Sharing need not be done the same way every day.

Mr. P lets all his sixth graders share, but he takes note of the especially provocative ideas thrown out. After all contributions are made, he refers to his notes and suggests further discussion of certain ideas. Sometimes he begins the discussion immediately after the contribution; sometimes he waits until another day. When the discussion is completed, he encourages follow-up through independent creative work.

Ms. C takes time during the first ten or fifteen minutes of the day to circulate among the various tables and listen to the children's conversations. She selects certain children for general group sharing so that over a period of time all children will have the opportunity to speak before the whole class.

Ms. F sometimes allows the children to share among themselves in three or four small, informal groups. Each group chooses one person to report later to the whole group.

Ms. R uses a screening committee of children who circulate among the groups and plan the next day's sharing period, selecting volunteers ahead of time. The committee chooses a particular topic for sharing or leaves the period open to any newsworthy item. Every now and then the entire group goes over the criteria set up for newsworthy, interest-holding, and idea-gaining items. The committee keeps a record of topics and of volunteers to be used in the evaluation period.

Ms. D limits the number of children who share on a particular day. She keeps a list of names and dates of sharing, and everyone eventually gets a turn. Children with items that can't wait, of course, are "specials." Children who have had similar experiences share at the same time. This procedure gives Ms. D time for discussion and follow-up of the ideas presented. Sometimes she quickly locates pertinent illustrations in her picture file; sometimes she finds an appropriate poem to read; sometimes she or one of the children illustrates with chalkboard sketches or demonstrates in dramatic form.

Sharing often leads to further study or continued expression through art or writing. Sometimes a whole class may get involved as a result, sharing the drawing of individual impressions, the making of collections, the preparing of bulletin-board displays, and so forth. At times a small group might want to go further by preparing experiments, constructing models, or planning interviews for securing further information.

Teachers, if need be, may screen items for group sharing or select certain ones for extended discussion. However it is arranged, time for sharing needs to be planned carefully if it is to be used to extend thinking and provide new awareness for creative follow-through.

Planned Small-Group Study

Teachers in team-teaching setups have a special advantage in planning all kinds of small group experiences, both firsthand and vicarious. While one or two teachers work with children in the classroom, another can be available for taking a small group on trips, conducting special sessions, and having conversations and dialogues about personal experiences, shared events, and so on. Sometimes aides or parent volunteers can be used in this way to free a teacher to work more closely in directing small-group experiences.

SUPPLIES AND MATERIALS

All kinds of concrete supplies and materials are useful in creative independent activities. Paper of all sizes and textures, cardboard, pencils, crayons, arithmetic measures and devices, dictionaries, encyclopedias, story books, pictures, museum items, microscopes, flasks—all should be located in appropriate self-service areas where they can be available for use during independent activity time. Needless to say, homemade items and all sorts of "junk" can be even more challenging to the imagination than commercial materials. The world is full of things that can be gathered up for creative uses and used to extend available school supplies and materials.

Managing Supplies and Materials

Whatever the materials to be used, individuals need help in learning how to manage them economically and in orderly ways. Because individuals and groups vary in the amount and kinds of responsibilities they can carry at a time, teachers need to find the best way to help their particular groups take responsibility for managing materials.

When Ms. S introduces new materials, she discusses their management with the children: where to keep them, how to care for them, how best to use them. A committee is responsible for checking supplies and for individual care of the standard materials such as clay, colored chalk, construction and easel paper, drawing paper, textiles, metals, paints, and brushes. Materials are stored within children's reach so they can get what they want without having to wait for the teacher.

Mistakes in handling materials are expected as a normal experimental procedure, but everyone understands how reasonable mistakes differ from irresponsible waste. Whenever possible, the committee solves complaints and difficulties and keeps the supplies available and the teacher posted about needed replenishments and problems. Ms. S, of course, works closely with the committee to help them fulfill their responsibility. In this way children have practice in managing supplies that belong to everyone in the room.

Working with Materials and Supplies

While individuals should learn to use materials carefully and purposefully, they need also to feel free to explore materials without anxiety or fear of failures. Trial-and-error is part of the creative effort. Everyone must recognize that failure often precedes success and satisfaction. Self-confidence in handling materials experimentally is one of the inner resources to be developed. When teachers value the search above the discovery and value thinking above the thought (however useful discoveries and thoughts may be), they will deliberately help children to acquire confidence in handling materials for creative expression.

Introducing New Materials

In addition to creating an experimental attitude toward materials, teachers will want to introduce new materials continually for creative expression. There are times, of course, when a new material should be introduced formally and careful instruction given in its use. An expensive microscope would be such an item. Working with metals or planing wood might be another. In a "here's how" period the teacher or resource person (who may be a child in the room, a child from another class, an adult working in the school, a parent, or any interested adult) can demonstrate techniques for working with the material. Some children, because of their backgrounds, often can function as "teachers," sharing their more expert knowledge and skill with other children. Regardless of who serves as resource person, the emphasis on creative learning need not be lost. An entire group can explore open-ended questions like

What could you use this material for?

If you did this (fold the paper like an accordian), what could you use it for?

How could you use this material to show this (what an elephant is like)?

There are times when some individuals will ignore the new material unless helped to use it. Those with low frustration levels probably need more careful introduction to materials before difficulty arises. On the other hand, new materials casually introduced often challenge others to find for themselves ways to use the materials and discover uses that the teacher did not anticipate. Mistakes sometimes occur, of course, but the satisfaction of overcoming obstacles through their own effort may be worth the risk. Individuals who make interesting and unusual discoveries with new materials can be asked to share their results with the group during sharing or evaluation periods.

Without limiting possibilities for creative efforts, teachers can still give direct assistance when necessary. Ms. C has her own way of handling such moments with her first graders. If she has time just when the child is experiencing difficulty, she helps him see through his problem with a question like, "What are you trying to do?" If she is deeply involved with another child or group, she may ask the child to get help from another, more experienced child or wait until the evaluation period to ask for the group's help. If she recognizes the difficulty as a general one, she might say, "Perhaps I'd better plan to discuss that with the whole class tomorrow (or later today)." Thus she establishes the need for guidance and makes the time to follow up the problem.

WORKING COOPERATIVELY

These days teachers need not work alone in arranging experiences and materials for creative independent activities. Team teaching with

one or more like-minded teachers in open space or next-door arrangements, all day or part of the day, has become an exciting way to combine
teacher enthusiasm, know-how, and work efforts on behalf of children.

There are also specialists available, not to take over classes, but to
team with regular teachers in areas like music, reading, writing, movement, art, and so forth, to develop more materials and ideas for independent activities than one person working alone can do.

Parent volunteers, senior citizens, older students, school administrators, and others can be added to the list of resource people to be con-
tacted and invited to work cooperatively with the teacher from time to
time.

Adult help, of course, must not diminish children's own efforts. The
challenge is to expand the range of experiences, materials, and techniques
at children's disposal, yet avoid interference. Children need to work their
problems through on their own in their own time. Their work should
reflect not the adult's thinking but their own capacity as creative beings.

The challenge for teachers, of course, is to make sure children are
reaching out, ever more confidently, to express their creative thoughts
and feelings more deeply, and are increasingly able to manipulate a range
of materials and techniques for themselves. The aim is to help children
grow steadily in both their creativity and independence. In this way, they
learn to teach themselves while also enjoying the process of using supplies and materials for creative purposes.

TEACHER PLANNING

It takes time to instill the habit of independent and productive
thinking/producing, but the teacher who believes in the importance of
creative growth will gladly take the time necessary to encourage it and
will deliberately plan for it to happen. The process begins with long-term
planning and broad goal-setting which then become the basis for developing short-term weekly and daily plans.

Long-Term Plans

Professional reading, curriculum guides, and experience over the
years suggest many vital goals toward which to work with a group. The
teacher can cull those most pertinent for a particular group. Ms. J made
her own list after going over her files of professional reading notes, the
district's courses of study, conversations with other teachers, and observations of the children in her group. Part of the list looked like this:

Civic responsibility, as a group member and citizen
  Practicing living in a democracy
  Assuming responsibility for contributing to the welfare of the democracy
  Assuming responsibility for preserving ideals of democracy
  Handling ideas and concepts
  Understanding what freedom means
  Thinking
  Using words correctly
  Expressing oneself
Self-realization, as a person
  Solving problems
  Getting satisfaction out of learning to help oneself
  Increasing independence in exploring interests and ideas
  Joining others in creative play
  Enjoying art, literature, rhythms, and music
  Developing body control and strength

Mr. P used courses of study to suggest his own list, recording some desirable behaviors for individuals in a democracy such as

Having a wide variety of interests and skills
Assuming social responsibility for use of time
Recognizing responsibility to keep physically, mentally, and emotionally sound
Working to reduce barriers between people
Becoming comfortable with oneself and others
Accepting problems of others as real and worthy of concern
Becoming sensitive to resources available for solving problems
Withholding judgment until all available facts are gathered
Assuming responsibility for making oneself understood
Working to understand viewpoints of others
Working to increase free flow of information
Weighing possible choices in terms of personal satisfaction and group welfare
Making long-term plans for use and conservation of resources
Making effective use of money for maximum benefit to oneself and others.

Ms. B simply kept a list of all possible curriculum areas and subject-matter skills. Every month or so she referred back to the list to check things out and decide on new things for emphasis the following month.

Weekly Plans

Broad goals often need to be broken down into more definite plans for a series of days or weeks. Ms. B made a plan chart each week to guide her. A few days of her block plan can be seen in Figure 2.3. With a block plan or plan chart in mind, Ms. B found it easy to jot down

FIGURE 2.3: Weekly Plan: Sample of Three Days.

MONDAY	TUESDAY	WEDNESDAY
Planning for day. Sharing news and happenings. Disc. Columbus Day. Read Alice Dagleish's **Columbus Story.** Brainstorm project ideas.	Discuss progress of Columbus D. projects and others.	Current events. Discuss letters/posters needed for Save the Animals drive. Plan rest of day. Explain new art technique to go in art center: tissue paper painting.
Indep. Activs. & Columbus Day projects. Meet with sm. group for reading compreh. practice. Use sea poems, Masefield (Sea Fever) and R. L. Stevenson.	Start wind study; list questions asked, get interest gps. going.	Indep. Activs. and wind-up of Columbus D. projects for afternoon sharing.
Work with K's group: root words w/suffixes: ly,y,ed. Help J's gp. find reference materials on Columbus.	Indep. Activs. Work with C's gp. to show how to use index in locating materials.	Meet with gp. studying spices then with gp. doing wind experiments.
Relax with music and snacks.	Work with S's gp. on spelling homonyms.	Snack time. Read and pantomime Rosetti's "Who Has Seen the Wind," and others from **Poems to Sit Still For.**
Read chapter from **Hobbit.**	Conference with individuals writing—try to extend thinking & build longer stories.	Share Columbus Day projects. Enjoy!
Prepare for camera walk. On return chart poem inspired by trip. Work out choral reading.	Relax with music and snacks. **Aesop Fable** gp. to dramatize fables worked on.	Read chapter from **Hobbit.**
Indivzd. Math: games & card files of problems. Conference with G's group.	Discuss trade routes of early explorers. Make 4 gps., each w/globe to check out continents, oceans, countries, etc.	Check out idea of class newsletter. If goes, brainstorm contents and divide jobs to be done.
Sing favorite songs.	Indivzd. Math: Work with gp. on division concept w/Cuisinnaire Rods.	Plan for tomorrow. Evaluate day.
Evaluate day.	Play records for rhythm band instruments.	
	Evaluate day.	

additional notes for each day's activities. Of course, at times a week's plans stretched into two weeks or changed for one reason or another. For one thing, each day's happenings provided diagnostic clues for next steps in teaching, and these frequently affected the next day's plans. Also, children's suggestions and ideas often became the nucleus of planning, sometimes for that day or the next day, sometimes for the following week. Consequently, while Ms. B's plans served as helpful guideposts, they were not viewed as inflexible.

Ms. H and Mr. P, team teachers for an older group of children who worked with an integrated-day plan, prepared a weekly chart to suit their purposes, with a sample morning plan. A sample week is shown in Figure 2.4.

Daily Plans

Daily plans need not be elaborately made nor follow a rigid form and style. One team-teaching group working with younger children made its daily plans in conjunction with weekly plans, simply listing on a chart what the children were to experience, if not on one day, then another, according to individual or group choices and needs. The charting looked like the one shown in Figure 2.5. Specific notes drawn from weekly plans, briefly jotted down, can remind the teacher of special items and schedules. But the teacher interested in promoting independence does not simply plan for children, but *with* them. Because everyone has a stake in the results, planning should be a cooperative venture.

STUDENT PLANNING

Although the teacher has special responsibility for planning, students have much to contribute to the process. Their goals, ideas, and suggestions can be used to enrich group thinking. Under the teacher's direction, children learn the skills of cooperative planning, both short-term and long-term planning.

Cooperative planning gives practice in learning to share responsibility in making suggestions, evaluating accomplishments, and improving conditions for creative work. Students who have helped to think through and carry out plans for scheduling time for work, arranging spaces for activity and managing materials for productive use are likely to understand what they are doing. They are also likely to function intelligently in selecting independent activities appropriate for their own growth needs.

FIGURE 2.4: Integrated Day Plan for Week of May 6.

TIME	*TUESDAY	WEDNESDAY	THURSDAY	FRIDAY
8:55–10:00	Discussion of trip and plans for project work	Total group meeting in auditorium for general communication and class organization work		
10:00–10:20	J U I C E B R E A K			
10:20–11:25	**GROUP A: Museum trip project work and follow-up activities GROUP B: Individualized reading/small group skills study GROUP C: Science—observation skills (mealworms)	GROUP C: Art—using perspective	GROUP A: Math—estimating GROUP B: Science—special interest group (reptiles) GROUP C: Individualized reading/skills	Class government organization work: Group D: Constitution Group E: Bill of Rights Group F: Elections Group G: Leaflets
11:30–12:00	Independent explorations in art, music, math and other areas Sharing morning's work/listening to story or records/ dramatics/movement			
1:00– 2:00	GROUP A: Individualized reading/skills study GROUP B: Language—poetry GROUP C: Language—writing books	GROUP B: Language—choral Independent explorations	GROUP A: Music—developing scale with bottles GROUP C: Individualized reading/skills study	
2:00– 3:00	Evaluations, sharing/clean-up/group meetings/songfest/rhythms			Progress reports

*Monday—Field trip planned to Fine Arts Museum.
**Groups A-G to be formed by self-selection, invitation and/or rotation.

FIGURE 2.5: Daily Plan for Six- and Seven-Year-Olds, Week of February 7, Mornings.

8:30-9:45	10:15-11:30
Mon., Tues., *Thurs., Fri.	

8:30-9:45	10:15-11:30
A. Group planning and interaction relative to individual reading activities	A. ⟶
B. Individualized reading	B. ⟶
C. Teacher-student conferences and guidance in book selection.	C. ⟶
D. Implementation of skills necessary to reading on an individual and group basis	D. Developing and extending listening skills, using
E. Book sharing and reading for those who have finished their reading and writing	1. Listening posts
	2. Small-group presentation of puppet shows
F. Development of individual active reading vocabulary stressing descriptive words	3. Individual science demonstrations (from older group)
G. Development of original stories based on individual reading and interests	E. Gardening group
	1. Planting
H. Making of books relevant to individual stories	2. Maintaining gardens
	3. Research, writing, reading as related to gardening activities
I. Discussion group follow-up of field trip to Travel Town and/or Tapia Park nature walk, sharing, relating, and categorizing ideas	F. Skill development for individual reading, writing, etc.
	G. Dramatization
J. Art activities as related to projects and field trips	1. Story reading or telling by teacher and students
K. Math activities	2. Development of stage setting and media for presentation
	3. Casting of characters
	4. Free interpretation
	5. Evaluation and discussion
	H. Science exploration by groups and individuals
	I. Construction and art activities in relation to individual projects and interests
	J. Spanish study and activities

*Wed.: There will be a field trip—Tapia Park nature walk. This will serve as a foundation for further activities and development in reading, language, and science.

Daily Plans

The daily planning session offers an excellent time to encourage creative thinking and responsibility for scheduling time, space, and materials for creative independent activities. There are certain questions that teachers can ask to help individuals plan creatively:

Have we included all the items we intend to do today?
Is there another suggestion?
How will that suggestion help us?
Does anyone see a problem we need to anticipate?
Are we planning toward our larger goals?
Are we getting balance in our plans? If not, how can we?
Are we trying to do too much today? Not enough?
Are there any questions?

Ms. F writes the daily plans on the chalkboard as the group makes them. In this way everyone knows the jobs and responsibilities for the day and checks on accomplishments. One day's cooperative planning looked like this:

Plan the day
Decide on individual responsibilities
Get committees started on research
    Space group: locate materials
    Pioneer group: work on mural
    Animal group: read references
Practice riddle making
Read independently and work independently
Learn a new game
Practice number combinations in groups
Evaluate the day

In Mr. H's room the day begins with a discussion of the plans for the day. Necessary responsibilities are listed, sequences of group experiences determined, problems of room management discussed briefly, and important items put on the agenda for the evaluation period. Mr. H shares with the group some plans that he has made as a result of his observation of pupil performance and needs for current projects. His discussion includes

Introducing some new art materials and techniques that might be useful for a social studies committee

Indicating that some children need direct teaching in the skill of
locating words in the dictionary
Identifying a group of children who need practice in adding long
columns of two- and three-place numbers

Whatever it is, he uses this time to share his thinking concerning the
group. He also uses this time to orient small-group work, preparing the
way for any seatwork responsibility or test situation he may wish to use.
Individuals add their ideas, share suggestions, and raise questions and
problems they wish to have the group consider. Jason may remind the
group that they have to change monitors for the week; Donna may
suggest that each reading group prepare a play for Washington's Birthday; Beth may ask if the tape recorder is available for use; Kenneth may
ask for help with an anemometer he is building; Jim may suggest that the
group study the community's highway problem; Allison may note that no
time has been provided for evaluation of the playground situation.

Some teachers prefer planning at the end of the day when the group
evaluates the day's accomplishments. New needs that come to light
during evaluation sessions can be included in plans for future work.
Sometimes groups block out plans for several days' work at a time, or for
an entire week. Ms. R appoints a planning committee to take charge of
writing the group's plans on the chalkboard daily and weekly, then
checking them off when accomplished. Goals for the day may be listed
briefly:

Committees finish research
Shelter Committee report
Notebooks
Individual work

Goals for the week may be presented at greater length:

Plan for the week
Continue discussion of what freedom means
Work on individual reading
Skills practice groups:
    Multiplication problems
    Liquid measures
    Phonics—word endings
    Oral reading
    Using indexes
Practice ball throwing and catching outdoors
Work on rhythm patterns for baseball story in music

Share individual work
Evaluation

Ms. F, during Friday's evaluation period, calls for suggestions for the following week's goals and activities and lists them on a wall chart to be used the following week in planning the class's daily schedule. During discussion the teacher suggests independent activities for the day. On another chart, she writes down: On your own

>   Make a painting or movie-story of Flag Day
>   Work in a self-service area
>   Make a collection for an exhibit of flags
>   Finish stories and pictures of vacation safety

With younger children, plans are stated simply and usually recorded by the teacher. Mr. S records plans on chart paper as he and the group discuss the day's activities. One day the chart read

Today we will—
>   Work on our stories
>   Read about Flag Day
>   Play catch outdoors
>   Listen to Dan's record
>   Finish our number sheet
>   Sing favorite songs
>   Talk about vacations

Whatever the procedure, daily planning sessions set the stage for working efficiently and responsibly throughout the day.

Long-Term Plans

Long-range student planning gives individuals direction as well as clearer understanding of the purposes for learning. Older children especially can be helped to take long-range views of their work. Ms. R and her sixth graders one month listed the creative jobs to be completed. The chart read

Things to Complete Before June 12
   1. Weather station
   2. Newspaper for community
   3. Social studies workbook
   4. Autobiographical stories including the future

5. Class work on human relations study
6. Long term papers
7. Categories for science display
8. Program for promotion exercises
9. A painting for the room display

Ms. D and her group list on the board their weekly goals, basing the daily plans on them. Ms. C titles a wall chart, "Things We Want to Do Next Week," to which items are added as suggestions and needs arise. Ms. F, at the beginning of the year, has the group think through goals and plans for the year. These are recorded; then each month they become the basis of an evaluation period to check progress. By having a share in determining what needs to be done and why, children can learn to feel a sense of personal satisfaction in accepting their responsibility to work independently in creative efforts.

RESPONSIBILITY OF THE TEACHER

Teacher/pupil planning should imply neither that individuals plan alone, with the teacher being simply a figurehead, nor that the teacher dictate all plans with the group merely listening and nodding. On the contrary, teacher/pupil planning is a two-way street in which both learners and teachers contribute according to their ability and sense of responsibility.

Children have the right to express and follow through current interests which they may have; they have the responsibility for planning goals and activities. Being human, they are subject to impulses and whims that need to be recognized. Nevertheless, teachers have their rights and responsibilities too. As curriculum experts in their classroom, teachers cannot rely completely upon individual whims or current interests, however useful they are. Instead, they should weigh all possibilities for creative learning and take an active leadership role. This may mean developing new or extended experiences; clarifying more efficient working procedures; or explaining new techniques and skills as needed. The alert teacher looks for all kinds of clues to individual needs by observing mistakes and problems that occur as students work creatively to express themselves.

As chief administrators in the classroom, teachers do not delegate total responsibility for planning a balanced program. In every classroom organized for quality learning, there should be a variety of ongoing activities designed to meet different purposes:

Time for small groups with similar abilities and interests to work
  together on problems and challenges
Time for friends to work together in committees or informal meet-
  ings
Time for wholegroup experiences of extended and new learning
Time for individual creative efforts with open choices
Time for thinking
Time for recording thoughts
Time for testing and diagnosing learning needs

As guidance workers in the classroom, teachers observe continually
in an effort to understand the ongoing behavior of children. They may
notice, for example, activities that motivate one child toward creative
power do not entice others, or activities that seem like easy choices to one
child look like hard ones to another. Because individuals differ so, the
same symptoms of behavior often carry different messages for guidance.
One individual who chooses the same activity repeatedly may be developing a talent; another may be compulsively expressing fear of failure
and lack of self-confidence in refusing to attempt unfamiliar tasks. Still
another may simply be showing unawareness of new possibilities. Dis-
covering why they choose as they do gives the teacher necessary clues for
better planning in meeting individual growth needs.

Studying students in order to uncover what *they* think and feel and
know is an important part of the teacher's responsibility in organizing the
day for effective learning and thinking. In their own ways, children
reveal what they need for creative growth:

Time to pursue independent activities on their own with a minimum
  of adult interference and a maximum of adult encouragement
Space, physical and psychological, in which to work in comfort and
  with confidence
Experiences that stimulate new thoughts and awarenesses as idea
  sources
Supplies and *materials* that provide the means for expressing ideas
Working cooperatively to enhance self satisfaction in being creative
  thinkers and producers

By organizing the school day for creative learning, the teacher provides the group members with freedom to make choices and stimulation
to work productively. These conditions imply the daily presence of a
wide range of independent activities that focus on the creative processes
of searching, organizing, originating, and communicating.

Chapter 3
Independent Activities: Searching

Activities that require *searching* for information open up new vistas of thought and extend current interests. They are appealing to students, for they offer a sense of adventure. Being fairly uncomplicated, even freewheeling in some ways, searching activities also provide easy success, whatever the individual's ability level and talents. Not only do they expand understanding and clarify ideas, they also stimulate the use of literacy skills, such as reading and writing, in functional settings.

Everyone from time to time confronts situations that seem confusing and seem to have no quick answers but invite searching, at least for understanding, if not for answers. Searching does not require discovery of "the answer," only the seeking of understanding. What matters is not that others know the answers, but that the searchers find answers for themselves and arrive at their own understanding. By actively searching, students gain confidence and power in their own ability to pursue questions and problems. They learn that understanding grows; there is always more to know, new problems to solve and old ones to reencounter. With a searching attitude, individuals learn to view problem solving as a great lifelong adventure; they keep their zest for asking questions: Why? What? How? When? What if? What then?

These questions begin early in life and, unless squelched, do not stop at the school doorstep. A well-balanced curriculum of a modern school should keep them going. With daily encouragement, children search for answers to their own questions, following their own hunches, identifying their own problems, and examining materials of their choice. In searching, they practice many skills and handle a variety of data sources, only one of which is reading. Others include picture searching, people interviewing, and phenomena observing. To overemphasize reading, especially through the use of a single textbook, confines searching to a limited, unchallenging experience. There is no creative challenge in knowing with certainty where needed information can be found. Nor is there creative challenge in searching for answers to teacher-made questions assigned as required seatwork, unless they are open ended and freely accepted as a personal challenge. The true challenge lies in being stimulated to search widely for satisfying answers to questions and problems important to the searcher. No searcher is too young or too old for this.

The sampling of searching activities presented on the following pages emphasizes what students might do on their own to experience creative searching in the school and classroom setting. Also included are suggestions to teachers for stimulating independent searching activity or for following up to encourage further development. The examples have been divided into three groupings: researching, sensorimotor exploring, and 3-R's searching.

RESEARCHING
Learning Areas 1-6

Researching is not a search activity reserved for adults who work as scientists. It is for inquirers of all ages who have questions they want answered for which they are willing to carry on a search with some degree of self-discipline. It starts with questions—the individual's questions—which lead to a search for answers. The results may not be sophisticated or generalizable, but the process will be experienced as a research investigation if done in a systematic way with a sharply defined question and hunches used to guide the search.

Researchers may study print, pictures, objects, environment, people, and so forth and practice basic skills such as

Observing closely
Listening attentively
Identifying content appropriate for their purposes
Relating what they see, hear, and read to their intentions
Noting details and evidence
Taking notes
Preparing and using questionnaires and survey forms
Using reference materials including maps, films, pictures, and real
    objects

The teacher helps, of course, but does not shortcut the process of searching that children must do for themselves as "researchers."

Learning Area 1. Interviewing

Subject Areas: Language Arts/Social Studies

STUDENTS

1. Interview various career and job people for a class study. These may be school workers, professionals, artists, business and tradespeople, factory workers, and so forth.
2. Interview classmates for talk times on improvised radio and TV shows or for a school newspaper column. Subjects might include

> Favorite foods, colors, games, sports, or computer programs/operations
>
> Places to visit, future plans, books to read, hobbies, heroes
>
> School rules, discipline and punishment, discrimination

TEACHER

• As questions arise on topics and problems, the teacher suggests interviewing people as a way to get answers. Students might write down questions of importance to them or dictate them to the teacher, who lists them on the board. Individuals and small groups then share responsibility for conducting the interviews and bringing results back to a class discussion.

• Discusses with the group some techniques for interviewing and arranges for trial practice if necessary. Also shows how questions can be put into an interview format for orderly information gathering.

• Helps students to realize the pools of knowledge and opinion sources waiting to be tapped through talking with people in interviews.

Learning Area 2. Surveying

Subject Areas: Social Studies/Language Arts/Mathematics

STUDENTS

1. Make classroom counts for a graph on
        Books enjoyed by boys compared to girls   TV watched
        School subjects most or least liked   Games played
2. Prepare inventories or pictorial surveys using snapshots or sketches of
   school and community problems needing attention. These might be
        Equipment or space arrangement
        Traffic conditions or land use near the school
        Appearances of empty lots
3. Prepare surveys on social issues, such as racial, sexual, age, or ethnic
   discrimination patterns found in the work community, for class discussion or presentation to interested organizations.
4. Put information about classmates into the computer, then use to get
   counts on
        Favorite dessert   Favorite color
        Favorite toy   Favorite season
   This can be graphed and displayed on printouts for sharing.

TEACHER

   • Helps to pinpoint plans for conducting a simple survey, using
questions and observation guides for collecting data in a useful form.
   • After individuals, working on their own, have collected information, the teacher, if needed, shows how to summarize the results on
graphs and charts that can be used for class discussion and possible
action.

```
                        BOOK SURVEY FORM
        _____BOY            _____GIRL          _____AGE

    1.  DO YOU LIKE ADVENTURE STORIES?        _____YES      _____NO

    2.  DO YOU LIKE POEMS?                    _____YES      _____NO

    3.  WHICH DO YOU LIKE MORE?     _____

    4.  DO YOU LIKE TRUE STORIES?            _____YES      _____NO

    5.  DO YOU LIKE MAKEBELIEVE STORIES?     _____YES      _____NO

    6.  WHICH DO YOU LIKE MORE?  _____

    7.  OF THE FOUR, WHICH DO YOU LIKE BEST? _____
```

Learning Area 3. Researching with Printed Matter

Subject Areas: Social Studies/Language Arts/Reading

STUDENTS

1. Search in books, pamphlets and computer data files for
     Information on a research problem
     Interesting songs or poems to learn
     Interesting facts and figures
     Information on personal collections
   These can be shared in discussions or used in individual project work.
2. Search through reference materials and catalogs to identify the variety of knowledge sources. These include atlases, world record books, almanacs, dictionaries, film catalogs, pamphlets, and directories.
3. Search for variations, contradictions, biases, and prejudices presented in written materials, to share in a reading circle discussion. Even two versions of a folk tale or news story can be used for comparison.
4. Search through newspapers and news magazines to find interesting current events for a bulletin board or class sharing.

TEACHER

   • Gathers all sorts of books and materials useful for researching on a class topic, including reading materials that have been tape-recorded so children can listen and follow along, if reading is a difficulty. Provides forms for recording interesting information, if needed, and arranges for sharing of results with classmates. Computer data files on a variety of topics add to the sources of data, when available.

   • Confers with individuals and small groups in order to identify topics and questions for researching and, later, to help process the information before sharing in class discussions.

Learning Area 4. Picture Researching

Subject Areas: Science/Social Studies/Language Arts

STUDENTS

1. Hunt for pictures that help to answer group or individual study questions. Sources might include

   Science and social studies textbooks   Files of prints
   Catalogs of slides and films   Magazines
   Photographs

   Tabs or markers can be placed in pages or a reference form filled out.

2. Collect interesting pictures, cartoons, or picture parts for a
   Scrapbook of images, with captions and labels
   Picture file of story-writing ideas
   Current-events discussion

3. Find photographs for a bulletin board. Topics might include
   Family histories
   Land changes (aerial photographs are useful here)
   Community changes
   Children's books

TEACHER

• Keeps picture resources available to students, arranges for library and museum loans, and encourages class collections of photographs and snapshots.

• Recognizes picture searches as a valid way of getting information and sees picture reading as an important study skill.

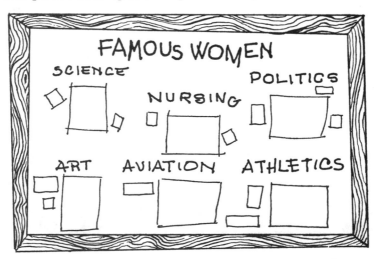

Learning Area 5. Researching with Real Objects

Subject Areas: Social Studies/Art/Science

STUDENTS

1. Examine art objects, such as
   > Masks, sculptures, drawings, paintings
   > Pottery, drinking vessels, batiks, mosaics
   > Literary films, children's books
   > Architecture of buildings

   These may become topics of conversation for small- or large-group discussions, or serve as ideas for children's own work.
2. Examine artifacts, costumes, old maps, tools, and other objects as a topic of class study and list questions to use for later researching with print, or simply make guesses about these items as a fun way to share and discuss with the class.

TEACHER

• When working with a class study topic or group theme, arranges to have various real objects available for examination. Students often have objects—old and new—at home that they can bring to school for display. Museums and other agencies, too, often lend out materials or welcome class groups for visits.

• Real objects serve a useful purpose. As first-hand materials they stimulate questions and wonderings, as well as all kinds of educated guesses. While authentic art objects are sometimes hard to procure and need to be handled carefully, they offer invaluable information and opportunity for searching. Reproductions and models often work as well.

Learning Area 6. Observing Scientifically

Subject Areas: Science/Social Studies/Language Arts

STUDENTS

1. Examine items on the science table and make hunches about properties, functions, structure, or origin before verifying by reading.
2. Compare sizes, shapes, and weights of objects for a class record chart.
3. Observe plants and animals to note movements, behavior, environmental conditions, and the like. Students might want to prepare a
   picture chart or diary by which to compare observation results with
   one another.
4. Make scientific observations by using apparatus such as

Microscopes	Electrical batteries	Computers
Prisms	Hand mirrors	Microcomputers
Magnets	Magnifying lenses	

TEACHER

• Makes sure that a science table or center is changed regularly and
includes both materials and specimens for close examination. If needed,
leading questions and direction cards may be added to help individuals
to look more carefully.

• Provides time for individuals to observe both natural and human-
made phenomena and to share discoveries.

• Makes sure that individuals recognize the power of observation as
a basic means of scientific inquiry.

SENSORIMOTOR EXPLORING
Learning Areas 7-14

Obviously, we learn by using our senses—all of them. It's our way of searching out what the world is really like and gathering for ourselves firsthand information. As we make contact and interact directly with objects and beings in the environment, we practice sensorimotor intelligence, gaining impressions and awareness in firsthand ways. In sensory searches, we learn to look more intently, listen more discriminatingly, smell more acutely, taste more carefully, and hold and touch with more feeling.

Children, in particular, need only to be encouraged to try sensorimotor searches and stimulated to use their senses freely in an ever-expanding range of possibilities. Access to many materials that differ in shape, texture, size, and color and to open interactions with the natural environment should prevent the usual school problems of (1) depending too much on sight and sound to the exclusion of other senses and (2) using sight and sound in narrowly defined, too-contrived, and overcontrolled search settings. As this kind of searching has both nonverbal and nonlinear qualities to it, it makes good use of the right-brain modes of intuitive, metaphorical thinking and serves as a bridge to left-brain, verbal modes. Sensorimotor searches help to build a solid intellectual foundation for other kinds of creative searching activities; they also are emotionally satisfying and useful in developing a sense of self-trust.

Learning Area 7. Mechanical Searching

Subject Areas: Science/Language Arts/Technology

STUDENTS

1. Explore various machines to figure out how they work and explain to others. These might be: typewriters, teletypes, telephones, printing presses, calculators, or microcomputers.
2. Try out various tools, such as
   Garden tools   Plumber's tools
   Carpenter's tools   Electrician's tools
   Students can prepare scientific charts that explain functions or characteristics.
3. Take apart a mechanism like a clock, motor, or small engine to find out how it is put together, then try to reassemble it, reporting on the results.

TEACHER

• Provides space for "messing around" with mechanical devices. At times certain devices may be included as part of a class study center such as gardening or telephoning, and students given the opportunity to try out and investigate what they can about them. Charts and cards of discoveries can be prepared and questions listed for further searching.

• Understands that many children are mechanically minded and need opportunities to develop their talents, while many others need to handle machines, tools, and equipment as a way to move from concrete experiencing to conceptual levels of thinking.

Learning Area 8. Sensory Searching

Subject Areas: Language Arts/Art

STUDENTS

1. Make a sensory search using touching by
     Taking a blind walk with partners
     Preparing small boxes or plastic bags of objects for touching
     Touching animals (turtles, snakes, fish, caterpillars, gerbils)
     Using hands and feet to compare water temperatures, muddiness,
         strength, and so forth
   Children can express the results of their search by preparing display charts, painting pictures, creating art designs, or recording sensations in a book.
2. Gather foods for a smelling and tasting party. Items can include fruits, spices, vegetables, jello or pudding, peanut butter, and the like. Foods can be prepared into dishes and soups, for more smelling, tasting, and eating.
3. Find objects to place in clear plastic envelopes, which can be magnified on a slide projector screen. Objects might be
     Leaf and flower parts
     Insects, fur pieces, wood grains
     Seeds or vegetable pieces
   Individuals may later wish to make drawings of their observations for a book.

TEACHER

• Plans with the group to set up a sensing center where all kinds of sensing samples can be organized in small boxes, plastic bags or wrappings, bottles, or pasted on cardboard pieces. Materials for sensing often may be part of a science center, an animal center, even a cooking area, where charts and empty books invite students to interpret their discoveries.

• Takes time to enjoy individual reactions and discoveries in a non-judgmental manner.

Learning Area 9. Artistic Observing

Subject Areas: Art/Language Arts

STUDENTS

1. Observe the world from different positions and points of view:
   Being a toddler on the floor   Standing on a hilltop or table
   Being a cornered animal   Being upside down
   Ideas gathered can be used in dramatics or sharing sessions.
2. Tune in to people's behavior, faces, expressions, moods, body movements, and so forth, to get ideas for a story or sketchbook.
3. Look for interesting or memorable patterns, colors, textures, scenes, or objects, in preparation for an expressive activity. Items might be
   A grove of trees   Reflecting water   Fences
   Clouds   Ants at work   Bird flocks
4. Examine famous paintings or reproductions and try to appreciate the range of impressions, feelings, and images offered. Observations can be shared in a small talk group.

TEACHER

• Recognizes unique perceptions and nonobjective observations as important intuitive knowledge and accepts such observations as a valid basis for creative activity.

• Includes in an observation center materials that can be used for artistic as well as scientific searching, where students can choose to work objectively or subjectively with their discoveries. Sometimes short, imaginative films also can be used for artistic viewing.

Learning Area 10. Picture Taking

Subject Areas: Technology/Social Studies/Language Arts

STUDENTS

1. Search for objects to use to make a photogram. Objects that make good silhouettes on light-sensitive paper include

    Pocketbook items, coins, buttons

    Matchsticks, pieces of lace, forks, spoons

    Feathers, leaves, flowers, plastics

    Feet, hands, hair

(Silhouettes immersed in photographic fixing bath for a few minutes make permanent pictures, useful as illustrations for original stories.)

2. Search for unusual scenes to shoot with a camera:

    Trees, stumps, storage rooms

    Pigeons walking, sparrows bathing

    Human body parts, such as face, hair, hands

A portfolio can be prepared, with captions and stories, and used for a story-idea picture file or a group newspaper.

3. Explore how pinhole (or real) cameras work by taking different shots of scenes or images, varying the distances, angles, lighting, positions, and such. Discoveries can be recorded in a photographic guide book.

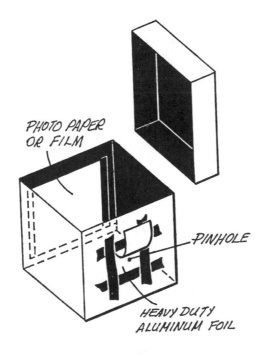

TEACHER

• Takes the group on a camera walk, where students search for something interesting to photograph, using a real camera, a video camera, or pinhole cameras.

• Provides photography books, how-to materials and instructions, along with a camera, video camera, or pinhole camera for students to examine. Students also may supply their own simple cameras. Sometimes a video camera can be borrowed, or the class may decide to embark on a money-making project to purchase or rent one.

• Arranges space where individuals can experiment with light-sensitive paper and pinhole cameras, or where, if and when chemical processing of prints is introduced, they can develop pictures.

Learning Area 11. Movement Searching

Subject Areas: Language Arts/Music/Mathematics/ Health/Physical Education

STUDENTS

1. Explore body movement with a partner or small group of friends, trying out

   Ways to sit and stand (stretching, bending, twisting, hunching, shaking)

   Ways to tighten and relax muscles (clenching and opening fists and faces, pushing and dropping shoulders)

   Ways to move with props (scarves, streamers, balloons, canes, hats, hoops)

   Results can be shared in presentations or sketch book and paintings.

2. Search for ways to use nonverbal comments, as in pantomiming a fable or poem, and shaping words or numbers.

TEACHER

• Provides space for physical adventures, both indoors and outdoors, along with props and activity idea cards for use in exploring body movement. Often these may be included in a musical or physical education center where there is equipment such as balance beams, hoops, drums, phonographs, and musical records.

• Helps students to appreciate movement exploration as a serious and disciplined yet joyful way of probing the natural flow of body power, grace, and energy. Movement searches often promote a sense of wholeness, as individuals discover what their bodies can do and say on nonverbal levels.

Learning Area 12. Sound and Music Searching

Subject Areas: Music/Science/Language Arts

STUDENTS

1. Search for interesting records, story tapes, songs, outdoor or indoor sounds, and so on, to add to a listening center or use for a small-group club session.
2. Form a rhythm band group to explore musical instruments, including self-made ones.
3. Conduct a search for sound differences and similarities among musical and nonmusical sounds, lullabies and marches, rock and jazz, voice ranges, and so forth. Results can be demonstrated or put on tape for use at a music center.

TEACHER

• Gathers with the group's help a variety of listening records, tapes, record players, tape recorders, earphones, musical instruments, song books, sound and music making materials, and musical compositions ranging from rock and folk music to jazz and classical. Instruments can include autoharp, recorders, bells, Chinese temple blocks, guitars, drums, shakers, tambourines, castanets, and many more.

• Since sound activities may create distracting noises, the teacher will need to help find appropriate places where children can feel free to work with sound in pleasurable, relaxed ways.

Learning Area 13. Finding Beauty in Things

Subject Areas: Art/Language Arts

STUDENTS

1. Search for pleasing poems, stories, and book illustrations to show and read aloud to a friend or to record on tape for a listening center.
2. Search through art books, art portfolios, libraries, or art museums for famous paintings and other art works to share with a friend or to use as inspiration for writing a poem.
3. Take walks to search for evidence of beauty in nearby places, both natural and human-made. Discoveries may be used in expressive activities such as painting, writing, creating a dance, or arranging a collection of small, gathered objects.

4. Collect beautiful natural objects and compose them into a three-dimensional, cardboard-framed "picture" or table centerpiece.
5. Find interesting human-made objects and examine them closely for appreciation of shape, texture, design, color, and functional quality. These might be
    Furniture or fixtures
    Books and baskets
    Implements such as scissors, straws, pencils, or tools
Individuals might search particularly for objects related to a class social topic and gather them for a display.

TEACHER

• Takes the group to the local museum or art gallery or on short nature walks, followed up by discussions and sharing of impressions. If the group is interested, helps to make plans to organize a class or school museum or art gallery on a theme of group interest.

• Encourages individual searches and collections for personal exhibits, as well as recordings in prints and paintings.

Learning Area 14. Finding Beauty in People

Subject Areas: Social Studies/Language Arts

STUDENTS

1. Share things they are proud of about themselves, in a small group.
2. Search for masks and clothing props, such as hats, shoes, costumes, and costume accessories, for a self-expressive Identity Parade.
3. Search through stories and personal experiences to find heroic human deeds to share in discussions.

TEACHER

• Helps the group set up an "Important Classmate of the Week" center. The individual selected can gather snapshots, mementos, toys, favorite objects, and so forth, for a "This is Me" display table. Classmates can take Polaroid snapshots of the student in action and share pleasant memories of personal interactions with that individual.

• Helps students to broaden their conception of beauty by learning to look internally as well as externally for signs of beauty in people. Suggests trying to express the searching in some tangible form that may be shared with others.

3-R'S SEARCHING
Learning Areas 15–21

Students often choose to practice 3 R's through searching activities. They search for words, stories, language structures, mathematical formulas and patterns, and the like. In the process of searching, they gain insights and skill in the various literary arts. Much of this kind of personally oriented searching can replace the structured assignments for practice that children often find tedious and impersonal. Here they can experience a creative search at the same time that they practice the traditional 3 R's.

Learning Area 15. Practicing Reading Skills

Subject Areas: Reading/Language Arts

STUDENTS

1. Search for instructions to follow in making something of interest, which then can be displayed for others to enjoy and use.
2. Find tongue twisters, riddles, jokes, quotations, or short verses to copy on the chalkboard or tagboard for others to read or answer. (Answers can be put in envelopes or on chart backs.) These also can be typed into a computer for screen reading and printouts.
3. Search for a good story or poems to
   Read aloud to friends, younger children, parents, senior citizens
   Arrange into a choral reading
   Use in an individualized reading program
   Read into a tape recorder, using the playback in evaluating and improving speech skills

TEACHER

• Develops with the group a simulated television or radio station center or reading center as a place for oral practice searches. Includes a tape recorder and changing assortments of read-aloud library books and readers.

• If the group is interested, helps to plan a choral reading program or session of favorite poems or stories to celebrate Library Week, Parents' Night, or some other occasion.

Learning Area 16. Using Semantics

Subject Areas: Language Arts/Social Studies

STUDENTS

1. Find emotionally arousing words for a personal word book on
    Sad and glad words   Important and unimportant words
    Liked and disliked words   Success and failure words
    Angry and kind words   Dull and exciting words
2. Gather one another's reactions and associations to typical words like *home, family, friends, happiness, school, play,* and *work.* The range of differences in feelings and perceptions found can be shared in a group.
3. Get together in a small group to talk about things liked and disliked and why (e.g., sport teams), to discover the kinds of values people have.
4. Find ads and other printed messages that show "straight" and "crooked" thinking, and share these in a small group. Students also might wish to develop an illustrated book on the hidden power of word messages.
5. Find words to add to class wall charts, with headings such as
    Slang Words and Jargon   Occupational Words
    Special Interest Words   Foreign Words

TEACHER

• During reading and writing conferences, calls attention to personal uses of words. Invites individuals and small groups to do semantic searches in learning the important relationship between language and human values.

• Includes opportunities to do semantic searching in a word or theme study center. Duplicated sheets of incomplete sentences, record books for listing examples and survey responses, photographs to examine for personal associations, and other ideas may be used to guide semantic searching. Results should be shared in discussions emphasizing the semantic nature of words.

 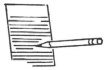

Learning Area 17. Personal Vocabulary Building

Subject Areas: Language Arts/Reading

STUDENTS

1. Brainstorm words on self-selected topics, using large sheets of chart paper or a blackboard. Lists can be categorized and used to accompany a picture file of story ideas, or in making picture scrapbooks.
2. Find synonyms, antonyms, rhyming words, puns, idioms, and so forth, to share in a small word-study group; use in preparing a thesaurus or language scroll.
3. Reread original or other stories to find interesting words to discuss with others or use in making up word games. These can be recorded on chalkboard or printed on tagboard strips or old computer cards.
4. Search for words, prefixes, suffixes, and other word structures to type into a computer, making lists for mixing and matching
    Compound words   New words
    Idomatic expressions   Synonyms

TEACHER

• Includes in a reading center a collection of helpful vocabulary reference materials, such as dictionaries, word books, glossaries, readers, and spelling books. A card file of activities pertaining to vocabulary building should be prepared.

• Shows interest in new vocabulary acquired by individuals, both in oral and written communication, and encourages doing independent word searches in a spirit of adventure and inquiry, not drill.

Learning Area 18. Practicing Spelling

Subject Areas: Reading/Spelling/Language Arts

STUDENTS

1. Search through plastic letter boxes, kept in a spelling center, for letters that
    Match or look alike
    Make interesting groups of letters and words
    Make anagrams, homonyms, or compound words
    These can be put on small flannel boards or in pocket charts, then shared.
2. Search through dictionaries, readers, or spelling books to find study words. These may be related to a topic, freely chosen or representing

particular word patterns being highlighted as a class search. Students can use the file to compile weekly spelling lists, keeping a balance between high-frequency words and specialty words.

3. Take an inventory of high-frequency or basic word lists to find words to practice for mastery. (Words can be prerecorded on tape or electronic devices.) Students should keep records that show their progress.

4. With a partner, search through computerized spelling word lists for words to spell. Sometimes software such as Wordman, Scrambled Word, and Spelling Wiz can extend the search.

TEACHER

• Presents inventories of basic spelling lists over a period of time to allow students to accumulate basic words as well as words from their own writing and personal searches.

• Helps to organize personal spelling books for individuals to use in accumulating words to study.

Learning Area 19. Practicing Handwriting Skills

Subject Areas: Language Arts/Spelling/Technology

STUDENTS

1. Find interesting words, syllables, or brief verses to practice on the chalkboard in cursive or manuscript handwriting; then have a friend or the teacher check for legibility.

2. Take a handwriting inventory and then select appropriate pages from handwriting analysis booklets for use in practicing in needed areas; practice on chalkboards, sand boxes, or paper. Postinventories can be used to check progress.

3. Write captions and titles in italics, calligraphy, or block lettering to go with posters, pictures, paintings, and word graffiti arranged for display. Students should practice these forms of handwriting with the help of guide booklets or resource experts.

TEACHER

• Includes spelling and handwriting practice in a word-study center, where materials such as handwriting practice booklets and alphabet cards can be kept. Provides practice space on blackboards or plastic-sheeted easels (for use with grease pencils).

• Encourages those who work on their handwriting skills to show results to others and discuss their progress.

Learning Area 20. Practicing Math Skills Using Calculators

Subject Areas: Mathematics/Language Arts

STUDENTS

1. Explore ways to use calculators by
   Checking answers or finding sums, products, quotients, and re-
   mainders
   Verifying computations and getting equations from answers
2. Make a calculator count by ones, twos, threes, tens, etc. If counts are
   made on tape, individuals can explore the printouts and share with
   others in a small-group math session.
3. Play calculator math games such as Calculator Bingo or others the
   group invents.
4. Use a calculator to
   Balance a checkbook
   Compute baseball batting averages
   Compare estimations with computer answers
   Recognize unrealistic computer answers
   Build shopping lists
   Verify a practice worksheet answer
   Experiment with operations relationships (following calculator
   guidebook instructions)

TEACHER

• Makes calculators, guidebooks, and card files of calculator activities available for individual and small-group independent exploration.

• Encourages individuals to record their searches and share discoveries. If the group is interested, helps to organize a banking or business
project centering around the use of calculators.

Learning Area 21. Computer Searching

Subject Areas: Mathematics/Technology/Reading

STUDENTS

1. Follow instructions for a simple computer program and examine mistakes in order to pick up clues to completing the program successfully.
2. Explore what happens when various keys are used during a program search.
3. Search for the computer's program secrets.
4. Search for a program of questions for others to work out (the instructor's booklet will provide operating instructions).

TEACHER

• Where there are computer terminals available or there is access to a computer center within easy distance, students should have the opportunity to explore computers. They can begin their search by attempting to follow instructions for completing a simple program, designed for elementary use. As they gain proficiency in handling a computer they can branch out to more complicated searching and begin to design their own programs.

• Sets up a computer workshop, arranging for a computer expert, or someone knowledgeable in working with computers and children, to lead the children through a series of beginning steps toward understanding how computers work. Encourages individuals and small groups to continue their exploration according to their personal interests.

Chapter 4
Independent Activities: Organizing

Some activities require more than searching. They require some kind of organizing, such as putting materials and ideas in a logical sequence, making classifications, or arranging information. Forms of arrangement vary from producing records to making and developing games, books, and stories. Organizing activities, like searching activities, generally appeal to learners. Results are tangible, and a sense of accomplishment is clear. Organizing activities also appeal to teachers because they promote practice in the use of thinking skills; among them are arranging ideas, synthesizing information from a variety of sources, and practicing logic in the presentation of ideas.

Learners face the challenge of organizing whenever they must pause long enough to pull together ideas, arrange information, and identify understanding and shape it into tangible form. This is what learning is all about.

In Piagetian terms, without assimilation and accommodation, without the opportunity, repeated endlessly, to structure and restructure knowledge for themselves, to make sense out of their explorations, children cannot experience true gains in knowledge or any true growth in intellect. There is no shortcut to the process.

Individuals must find out for themselves what they know, recognize for themselves what it means, and develop their own structure of accomplishment. As they do this by engaging in various kinds of organizing activities, they have the opportunity to think creatively, produce creatively, and apply a host of basic skills to their creative endeavors.

What counts here is the individual's organizing activity, not the teacher's. The teacher helps, of course, by avoiding use of prestructured, preorganized worksheets and workbooks that deemphasize creative thinking and organizing. In their place, the teacher provides a range of independent activities that call for creative organizing. Among the possibilities, seven categories stand out: Keeping records, organizing collections, making charts and maps, making games, organizing research information, extending the 3 R's, and extending common experiences. Each category that follows contains examples of independent activities for learners and suggestions for teacher guidance.

KEEPING RECORDS
Learning Areas 22-26

Keeping records can be a useful organizing experience in our daily lives. It helps us to evaluate our activities and become aware of personal progress. Recordkeeping also helps in tracking thoughts and reactions, and retrieving scientific and social data of interest. By keeping records, children learn to condense information to manageable size and use the data as a basis for further study and action. They practice skills like

Using a simple time sequence
Outlining by listing ideas in sequential order or by listing materials
    and books under a single topic
Selecting pertinent ideas from broader reading activities

As students experience the activity of recordkeeping, they begin to recognize the part records have played in social and scientific advancement. They grow to appreciate more fully the contributions of those who keep records: historians, writers, scientists, teachers, and others, including themselves.

Learning Area 22. Keeping Progress Records

Subject Areas: Social Studies/Language Arts

STUDENTS

1. Organize collections, including portfolios of artwork samples, musical compositions, original stories, poems and reports, snapshots of creative productions, computer printouts, and so forth. Over a period of time, keep a growth and accomplishments record to share with the class and parents.
2. Organize skills charts that can be used to check off progress and determine improvement needs in various skill areas.
3. Keep individualized reading records of authors, book titles, dates, and comments. Records might be in the form of paintings, paper scrolls, card files, reading wheels, charts and graphs, book jackets, and so on.
4. Contribute pages to various class progress record book projects, such as handwriting progress, trip records, or class yearbooks.
5. Contribute to an ongoing scientific record notebook or large, ringed data book that contains group observations from scientific happenings, such as

Plant growth	Computer discoveries
Weather changes	Environmental changes observed on weekly walks

TEACHER

• Confers with individuals, talks about their progress and accomplishments, and encourages record keeping as a way to gain objective appraisal data.

• Develops with the group an archives center where growth records can be stored and used for evaluation purposes until no longer needed.

• Keeps an assortment of class record books that need attention, so students can contribute to those they are interested in. Some class books may be made simply with poster-board sheets and a notebook ring; others may be prebound by the teacher or small group.

• For some students, contributing a comment, picture, or page to a class record book is an easy entry into bookmaking and a sensible introduction to reading and writing.

Learning Area 23. Making Self-Evaluation Reports

Subject Areas: Social Studies/Language Arts

STUDENTS

1. Fill out self-report cards to accompany the teacher's.
   My best subject is _____.
   The subject I need to work hardest on is _____.
   The subject in which I think I have improved the most is
   _____.

2. Fill out self-report cards to share with parents.
   MY WORK HABITS
   I try to correct errors.
   I ask for help when I need it.
   I read questions carefully.
   I can organize and keep track of my work.

   MY READING SKILLS
   I understand what I read.
   I understand math word problems.
   I take part in discussions.

   MY SOCIAL ATTITUDES
   I listen to suggestions.
   I try my best.
   I take good care of equipment and materials.
3. Describe personal accomplishments in class sharing periods around
   questions such as
   What did you do today or this week that helped you? that helped
      others?
   What new idea or skill did you discover today?

TEACHER

   • Stresses self-evaluation by helping individuals to identify a suitable
evaluation program. Various evaluation forms may be developed with
the group and used in conferences. Expects students to write freely about
their work in narrative form, to be shared with parents, teacher, and/or
the school principal.

Learning Area 24. Making Other Evaluation Reports

Subject Areas: Social Studies/Language Arts

STUDENTS

1. Fill out an evaluation report of the teacher.
   Dear Ms. _____:
   You have helped me most to improve in _____.
   I think you could help me more in _____.
   Your pupil, _____
2. Write or draw a report for parents on
   What we studied this week   Our plans for next week
   What we did in school today
3. Prepare opinion statements or drawings on a variety of topics and problems and use them to present points of view at class meetings on
   Controversial issues   Favorite reading or TV shows
   Consumer products   Class management problems

TEACHER

• Establishes with the group suitable class or individual topics for opinion gathering. Opinion statements can be written, drawn, or recorded in some way.

• Conducts periodic class meetings where individuals express opinions and personal judgments without risk of ridicule or rejection. If needed, helps students to learn appropriate ways of agreeing and disagreeing, to express views in some coherent way, and to feel free to change their minds, as they exchange opinions and judgments in open forum.

Learning Area 25. Keeping Diaries and Journals

Subject Areas: Social Studies/Art/Language Arts/Reading

STUDENTS

1. Draw weekly picture diaries in booklets or on charts, of
   School events or happenings at home   Computer discoveries
   Weekend activities or TV shows
2. Keep an illustrated journal for personal use or sharing. It may be on
   Thoughts and reactions to events
   Dreams and fantasies
   Imaginary characters living in other times or places
   Nature sketches and poems
   New ideas and questions related to a study topic

3. Contribute to a daily class log organized to identify what is being learned or studied about a topic. Topics can include social learning such as kind behaviors, being responsible, what freedom means; or class trips taken, whether short walks, long bus rides or overnight stays, telling where and why the class went, when and how, and what was learned.

TEACHER

• Promotes diary and journal writing as a major writing choice by providing journals, the time to write, and the option of sharing with classmates or the teacher.

• The class might like to keep a diary of some kind as a group project for a few weeks. For this the teacher takes dictation or appoints a secretary to record information in a large log book, which can be shown to parents when they visit.

Learning Area 26. Recording Scientific Discoveries

Subject Areas: Science/Language Arts

STUDENTS

1. Write or draw on forms headed "My Science Discovery" observations made

—in using:
    Magnets
    Globe
    Magnifying glasses
    Levers

—or in examining:
    Plants
    Human anatomy models
    Missile models

2. Organize chart records for science discovery books, showing findings made on research topics such as

    Weather or daily temperature changes
    Mineral products and their geographical sources
    Computer procedures
    Activities during a certain hour or day
    Historical events

TEACHER

• Prepares charts and booklets with ample space for individuals to record their discoveries. This information can be organized later according to topics or categories suggested by the group.

• Brings to the group's attention the importance of recording discoveries as a way of processing science and develops with the group various appropriate forms to use when gathering information.

ORGANIZING COLLECTIONS
Learning Areas 27–31

Making collections is a universal interest of childhood that often continues throughout life. We enjoy collecting objects and ideas, then putting them in order. The experience puts us in touch with the basic principle of an ordered universe. It also gives us something special to share with others. Well-organized collections not only add to the enjoyment of collecting but give us a basis for sharing and discussing with others for mutual learning.

In preparing collections, useful and interesting facts are gained and many skills practiced: planning, comparing, listing, categorizing, reading, writing, and decision making, among others.

By the choices of what to collect and how to organize the collections, individuals express their personal interests and abilities. They display their specialized areas of knowledge. Making collections helps the collectors absorb parts of the outer world into their own inner sphere to assimilate new knowledge. The activity deserves an important place in the daily school curriculum.

Learning Area 27. Making Classification, Information, and Experience Charts

Subject Areas: Social Studies/Science/Language Arts/Reading

STUDENTS

1. Make classification charts to organize information learned about a topic.
   Astronomy (planets, stars, moons, galaxies)
   Animals (sea, forest, jungle, desert)
   Tools (boat, building, auto, plumbing)
   Charts can be shared, then displayed on bulletin boards.
2. Make pictorial theme study charts by cutting out pictures or drawings and arranging them carefully on a large sheet of tagboard. Themes might be

Holiday Celebrations	City Life
Courtesies in Different Cultures	World Climates

3. Make instructional charts to use in reporting a study on

Places I Lived	Winners and Losers	Life Cycles
Long Ago and Now	Plants and Animals	Playing Safe
Big and Small	Making Applesauce	

4. Make charts to illustrate number meanings and concepts with such quantity words as gallon, dozen, dollar, hundred, more and less, large and small, and so on.

TEACHER

• Makes sure that there is ample opportunity for students to record their activities and learning on charts that communicate to others in expository ways. Supplies and chart paper might include cardboard sheets, posterboard sheets, newsprint sheets, butcher paper, felt pens, markers, and colored pens.

• Helps students to organize their learning in chart form using words, sketches, diagrams, and pictures. Arranges for completed charts to be shared with others and displayed for study.

Learning Area 28. Organizing Word Collections

Subject Areas: Language Arts/Spelling/Reading

STUDENTS

1. Choose words for a class spelling file, dictionary, or thesaurus. Words can be organized by
   Structure (compound words, homonyms, prefixes, suffixes)
   Function (action words, descriptive words, connecting words)
   Association (words that in one way or another belong together)
   Alphabetical or frequency order
   Use (occupational words, botanical words, historical words)
2. Collect words and illustrations to add to class phonetic wall charts. Each chart might emphasize a phonetic element like beginning consonants or blends, short or long vowels, endings, and so forth.
3. Cut words and phrases from magazines and newspapers to add to class word collections. If a classification system is used, place the words in the proper box.
4. Contribute to a class vocabulary study on different topics
Letter-writing words	Electricity words	Insect words
Hospital words	Election words	Space words
Environmental words	Machine words	Computer words
5. Create class graffiti of words to celebrate a special day, cause, or event such as
   Valentine's Day, Spring Celebrations, Veteran's Day
   Peace, conservation, elections
   Birthdays, outdoor education camp

TEACHER

• Provides collection boxes for words printed in various styles of large type that can be used to compose signs, posters, announcements, stories, and so forth. The words may be sorted into boxes according to topics, parts of speech, basic vocabulary, and unusual words, or any other system, depending on the students' maturity.

• Begins a large word chart for the class during a discussion, and has students search for words to add to the chart. At the end of the day, the chart can be shared and discussed.

• Conducts brainstorming sessions; has students suggest words on a topic recorded by the teacher on large sheets of newsprint. Later the group can discuss and categorize words and make plans to use them in individual and group activities.

Learning Area 29. Preparing Lists

Subject Areas: Social Studies/Language Arts/Science

STUDENTS

1. Make top-ten opinion lists to check out against others' lists. These can be songs, poems, books, athletes, famous women or men, or whatever.
2. Make a suggestion list to present for class discussion and action; for instance, preventing waste at home and in the community, or keeping peace in the world.
3. Learn to make computer lists. Collect information to type into the computer and request "lists," either of the total input or by category titles that also have been entered. Topics might include
   Story titles
   Leisure-time activities
   Chores

TEACHER

• Uses class study themes and personal interests to launch list making. Shows how lists can be made on paper strips, accordion-folded paper, posterboard cards, columned paper, and in other interesting forms that can be arranged on posters and bulletin boards for easy reading or put into book form.

• Brainstorms with the class various topics for making lists and from time to time gets the group involved in a class list-making project for a class anthology.

Learning Area 30. Forming Collections of Contrast

Subject Areas: Social Studies/Science/Language Arts

STUDENTS

1. Collect pictures or objects that illustrate contrast and use them for a scrapbook, picture file, or display table. Categories might be

Things that grow above and below ground	Manual and machine labor
	Sweet and not sweet foods
Things that fly and walk	Fruits and vegetables
Homes then and now	Heavy and light things
Domestic and wild animals	

2. Contribute to a class mural contrasting human conditions in need of attention, such as

war/peace	play/work	masculinity/femininity
freedom/slavery	rich/poor	happiness/sadness

3. Make a culture-contrast collection for a bulletin board, comparing customs, beliefs, language expressions, women's and men's work, and so forth.

4. Make illustrated contrast lists for a bulletin board or book of contrasts, on topics such as

Fact and Opinion	True and False
Noisy and Quiet	Summer and Winter
Then and Now	New York and California

TEACHER

• Builds vocabulary meaning by keeping some idea working in the classroom that gives individuals an opportunity to organize their information around contrasts.

• Sets up a leading question on a bulletin board, on a table space, or in a scrapbook and asks individuals to contribute pictures, ideas, or words to the collection. When the collection is large enough, a small group might present a report to the whole class, or individual students might make personal books.

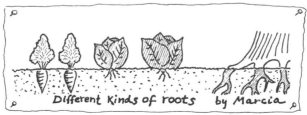

Different kinds of roots   by Marcia

Learning Area 31. Organizing Class Collections

Subject Areas: Language Arts/Art/Social Studies/Science

STUDENTS

1. Contribute specimens and objects to class collections, accompanied by labels and/or descriptive material:
   Uniforms, hats, equipment, costumes, photographs, old things
   Foods, texture samples, new inventions, musical instruments
   Buttons, leaves, minerals
2. Contribute to group collections for Parents' Night, such as
   Handwriting styles, art styles, crafts expertise
   Opinions on questions and issues, ideas and information on a topic
3. Organize an anthology of original stories or favorite poems, proverbs, riddles, jokes, and the like. Items can be pasted or copied into a scrapbook and illustrated.

TEACHER

• Capitalizes on the natural interest in collection making by providing places in the classroom where these "treasures" can be shared. A table can be designated for collections like baseball cards, stamps, shells, stuffed animals, recipes, coins, buttons, stickers, or other items that individuals might collect.

• Depending on individual maturity, the teacher prepares a guide for study of the collections and provides printed materials to use in making descriptions and classifications of observations. Magnifying glasses, a microscope, or other aids for study can be provided when appropriate.

• Helps students who have gained information about their collections to organize the information into a bulletin board display, book, or oral presentation.

MAKING CHARTS AND MAPS
Learning Areas 32-37

Making charts and maps provides the opportunity to develop not only mathematical, reading, and writing skills but also organizational and thinking skills. As students process data in pictorial, graphic, or scroll fashion, they structure an informational base for making generalizations, comparisons, interpretations, inferences, and even hunches for further study.

Making charts and maps offers the double advantages of bigness and brevity. Children particularly enjoy working with colorful pens and pencils on large pieces of tagboard, newsprint, or butcher paper when recording results to be displayed and discussed. They also like the idea of using a minimum of words and numbers and learning to work concisely in limited space.

Gaining practice in structuring their own charts and maps enables children to read those made by others more easily, with more understanding and perhaps with better discrimination.

Learning Area 32. Making 2-D Maps

Subject Areas: Social Studies/Art/Language Arts

STUDENTS

1. Paint a large background map-mural for a dramatic play center on
   Underseas world for submarine level   Hospital life
   Space travel   An enchanted forest
2. Make a special-purpose map, such as a
   Treasure map to show where a hidden object is
   Road map to show a trip route
   Street map to show property ownership and where people live
   Playground map to show how play space can be sectioned off
   Completed maps with appropriate key symbols can be placed in a map study center for others to read and discuss.
3. Make a large pictorial or specimen map with draw-ons or paste-ons showing local, national, or worldwide distributions of parks, animals, crops, climate patterns, population centers, and so forth.
4. Use a computer to draw a map, stars, an imaginary planet, or a new town, and use the printout to explain the item to the class.

TEACHER

• As individuals organize maps of their choosing, the teacher raises questions to stimulate more awareness of the basics of map making. Encourages sharing and displaying of results.

• Sometimes uses a field trip as a way to begin a class map project. Students might take snapshots or make drawings to use later in organizing a map-making project.

• Uses map making, not as an experience in reproduction (copying), but for the purpose of organizing and interpreting what has been learned.

Learning Area 33. Making 3-D Maps and Globes

Subject Areas: Social Studies/Technology

STUDENTS

1. Make a large floor or table model of an area actually walked through, then viewed from an elevated position. (Areas might be school-grounds, a business, or neighborhood center, or a park.) Streets can be painted on or laid on with kraft paper strips. Landmarks can be cut out of construction paper or thin cardboard.
2. Make map layouts with blocks or boxes used in dramatic play:
     Skyscrapers and bridges, roads, airports, harbors
     Farms, city streets, factories
3. Help organize a project to make a large world globe out of papier-mâché, inflatable material, or large, blue, beach balls. Emphasize features such as
     Mountains, continents, and deserts
     Air routes, exploration routes, and trade routes
     Countries, capital cities, and seaports
   The completed globe can be used for discussions and reports.
4. Help to organize a plaster relief or sand-table map on a study topic such as a river's story, a battle scene, or an historical site.

TEACHER

• Encourages individuals and small groups to make maps on their own to share with others or use in dramatic play and research studies.

• Ample floor or table space should be allowed for map making, and special outdoor areas designated for such purposes. Different materials can be used, including putty, plasticene, clay, sawdust and glue, salt and cornstarch, molding sand or plaster of paris mixed with water, and papier mâché on plywood, etc.

Learning Area 34. Drawing Graphs

Subject Areas: Mathematics/Science/Social Studies

STUDENTS

1. Collect and count interesting objects, sort and classify them by size, color, shape, types, and so on, and create bar graphs to reflect these categories and the items in them.
2. Organize bar, line, or picture graphs to show results of investigations on
     Number and kind of pets owned by classmates
     Number and sex of children in families of classmates
     Use of land surrounding the school within a one-half-mile radius
3. Make circle graphs to show distributions of
     Money collected from a paper drive for a school or community cause
     Tray/snack/bag lunches
     Daily class and group activities
4. Keep graphs showing improvement in spelling, math, or other skills.
5. Plot various single- or double-line graphs, bar graphs, or pie-chart graphs on a computer, using a software disk that permits such pictorial displays, such as "Bank Street Laboratory."

TEACHER

• During a group discussion and sharing of activities or preferences, the teacher suggests making a graph to show the information in a quantitative way. Works with the group to develop the graph and interpret the results.

• If individuals are interested, other graphs can be planned with charts or bulletin board space and appropriate headings to guide individual contributions. The teacher also should encourage individual and small-group graph making as data are collected on topics of curiosity. Computers, if available, lend themselves well to graph-construction activities.

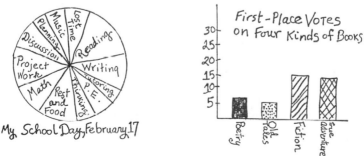

Learning Area 35. Making Flow Charts and Organizational Diagrams

Subject Areas: Social Studies/Language Arts

STUDENTS

1. Prepare flow charts of interesting processes to show others:
   Water cycles, salmon life cycles   Writing/book publishing
   House building   Baking cookies
   Space exploration   A number-guessing game

2. Make organizational diagrams showing structural setups of
   School safety patrol or public school districts   Family or clubs
   Local or federal government   Computer input

3. Make flow charts of interesting personal events to accompany oral
   sharing:
   The Day I Went Skiing   A Birthday Surprise
   My School Day of Bumps and Bruises   An Easter Egg Hunt

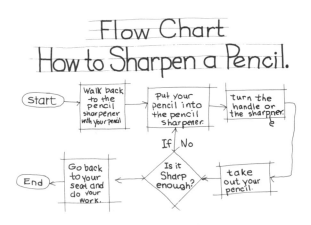

TEACHER

    • Works with the group to set up a chart related to a common interest area and then displays it as a model for students who wish to plan their own.
    • Brainstorms with the group possibilities for flow charts and organizational diagrams and then charts the ideas and directions for making them.
    • Gives time for class sharing and arranges for small-group sessions so students can teach others who want help in learning how to make the charts.

Learning Area 36. Setting up Statistical Tables and Matrices

Subject Areas: Mathematics/Social Studies

STUDENTS

1. Make tables of contents for original storybooks or class anthologies.
2. Make statistical tables of classroom data for group discussions:
   Daily attendance, by sex or age
   Games played most or least frequently
   Subjects best or least liked
   Times of day best or least liked
3. Make an information matrix on various research topics to use in reporting to the class, such as:

Games Played by Different Age Groups
Young kids _____
Older kids _____
Grownups _____

Other topics might be on how people feel about the weather, reading habits, and so forth.

TEACHER

• Introduces the idea of tables and matrices as part of a classroom investigation, helping the group to organize a table from the data gathered and using it for discussion. Encourages students to develop tables and matrices in organizing their own investigation results.

• Collects mathematical materials for individuals to use when computing data for tables. These might include small computers, calculators, percentage charts, and booklets explaining statistical information (means, modes, percentiles, number order, and so on) and giving directions for setting up tables and matrices, along with samples to follow.

How Children feel about School:

	☹	😐	😊
Primary Graders	20	30	35
Intermediate Grades	35	25	20

TABLE I

Games	Number of Kids
Tag	15
Dodge	10
Relay	5
Soccer	5

Learning Area 37. Inventing Codes and Symbols

Subject Areas: Mathematics/Music/Social Studies/Language Arts

STUDENTS

1. Create messages with new letter or number codes for friends to decode.
2. Make treasure maps with symbols and key codes for a map-study center.
3. Invent a musical notation system for a dance movement or song to be performed at a talent show.
4. Invent a new alphabet or hieroglyphic code to add to a word-study center.
5. Develop coded procedures for a computer to follow in creating a design or mathematical problem.

TEACHER

• Establishes an environment wherein individuals feel free to invent all kinds of symbols and codes and can come to realize that systems and codes are simply arbitrary but orderly setups created by people. Gives help as needed and arranges for results to be shared.

• At times, takes dictation for an experience chart written in hieroglyphics or a code suggested by the group. If interested, the class might brainstorm a hieroglyphic language, inventing code charts for individuals and small groups to use in developing their own hieroglyphic stories.

• Arranges for display of printouts that students have made, along with explanation of codes and symbols used.

MAKING GAMES
Learning Areas 38-41

Games made by students add challenge to fun. Constructing a game, even a simple one, requires awareness of detail, clear-sightedness of purpose, and careful organization if others are to understand and enjoy it. In addition to the learning involved for those who choose to create a game, the organizers also gain satisfaction as others use the game for learning and pleasure, too.

Challenging activities for fast learners include (1) making games that review skills in word recognition, arithmetic facts, science information, music reading, and spelling; (2) producing games of logic that require decision-making activities like classifying, serializing, inferring; and (3) preparing simulation games that try to recreate real situations and dilemmas. Playing the games may be less demanding on thought and creativity but worthwhile for reading review, recall, and application of strategy.

Game making and playing afford opportunity for mutual help and friendship in group living as well as for creative expression of individual needs. Individuals interact socially as they study directions, interpret rules, and bring out a game's possibilities. They learn to give and take in winning and losing, to arbitrate differences, and to recognize the importance of following rules. Games have a long history behind them of being invented, not merely for entertainment but to develop important skills and thought processes. They should be an integral part of classroom life.

Learning Area 38. Preparing Mathematical Games

Subject Areas: Mathematics/Social Studies

STUDENTS

1. Develop box and carton math games using materials, such as
   Graph paper for strategy games
   Disc flips, with math facts and numerals painted in egg-carton holes, into which contestants throw marbles or dice and add, subtract, multiply, or divide according to the rules they set up
   Dart boards with numerals to add, subtract, multiply, and divide, or with story problems to solve
   Bingo or game boards for a shoelace match game

2. Make cards of arithmetic facts to use in a game of their own invention.
3. Write a computer program for a math game to play with a friend. Dragons, space aliens, and alligators can be used in preparing games for math facts and equations.

TEACHER

• Provides general directions and suggestions for making math games, and makes available an assortment of cast-off materials, such as
Empty juice cans and coffee cans with plastic lids
Egg cartons, wood boards, heavy cardboard pieces or boxes
Plywood boxes, nails, paper clips, brads, and chipboard pieces
• Expects students to take responsibility for keeping their games both accessible and in good condition.

Learning Area 39. Making Classification Games

Subject Areas: Social Studies/Language Arts/Mathematics/Art

STUDENTS

1. Organize card games calling for matching or classifications. Pictures can be pasted or drawn on cards, or words printed on them of objects collected on a variety of things:
Animals and plants
Clothing for dress, work, play
Language equivalents
Related objects like table and chair, knife and fork
Raw and manufactured materials
Geography items like countries and continents, capitals
and states
Make up rules for the games and prepare labeled boxes or pocket charts to use in sorting.
2. Organize classifying and sorting games to be played on a computer.
3. Make up games to use in reviewing items studied in social studies and science:
Famous women and men
Products from petroleum
Cities of America
Rivers of the world
Sources of power
History of communication

TEACHER

• Cardboard, pictures, paints, and glue are among the materials that should be available for making games. Samples of commercially produced games will give children ideas for rules, format, and special materials. A brainstorming session should produce many ideas for games that would be useful as reviewing and recalling exercises.

• When a class is working with factual content, the teacher might help a small group to identify facts that would be suitable for a classification game and let the members develop it for class use.

• Games with a pattern of play that requires players to start at a given point and progress toward the "finish" by answering certain questions are another good way to get children to organize their information into sensible questions with brief answers.

Learning Area 40. Making Crossword and Cross-Number Puzzle Games

Subject Areas: Language Arts/Mathematics/Science

STUDENTS

1. Make puzzles on a theme idea or terms derived from
    Science or social studies
    Music or arithmetic
    Reading stories
2. Cut stencils and duplicate enough puzzles to give one to each class member.
3. Submit puzzles to the school newspaper for publication.
4. Include puzzles and answers in class magazine.
5. Create a computer-made puzzle from weekly spelling words. Software disks like Crossword Magic (available through Creative Publications) can be helpful as a guide.

TEACHER

• Crossword puzzle games, especially those developed around a certain topic, are activities that help students to establish a wide vocabulary and increase spelling skills. The teacher should bring to the classroom crossword puzzles from children's magazines and newspapers for individuals and small interest groups to use as takeoffs for organizing their own.

• The class can discuss requirements of a good crossword or cross-number puzzle, and as a group they can try to make one on the chalkboard.

Learning Area 41. Organizing Play Games

Subject Areas: Physical Education/Social Studies/Language Arts

STUDENTS

1. Take charge of developing a relay game in a four-step process:
   Plan (choose distances and relay objects; set up relay posts)
   Advertise
   Teach
   Monitor
2. Make up new variations for favorite old games, such as Capture the Flag, Simon Says, Freeze Tag, Musical Chairs, Red Light–Green Light, or Telephone.
3. Think up a new game for classmates to play. Establish rules and challenges, arrange for scoring, and determine the winner's rewards.
4. Organize a team game and take responsibility for coordinating it.
5. Contribute to plans for an events day. Organize, for example, tournaments, decathalons, bike days, skating days, and the like.

TEACHER

• Introduces a games project. If the group is interested, helps to plan desirable games and game activities, to organize work committees, and to divide up responsibility for launching the project. Discusses matters such as safety needs, the need for rules, and ways to increase cooperation and reduce competitiveness.

• Dialogues with the class about organizing outdoor games and game events or planning new games. Encourages dry runs to iron out snags before presenting to others.

ORGANIZING SEARCH INFORMATION
Learning Areas 42-43

Organizing information gained by searching becomes part of the challenge in showing results of study. It is an opportunity to follow curiosities and shape results in some ordered manner that can be shared with others and discussed. Thus, data that have been searched out become retrieved data; that is, they are recalled and reformed in a more condensed, concise way, different from the original sources. Having retrieved data makes it easier to do conceptual thinking and make generalizations or hypotheses. In this sense, retrieving search information becomes a reordering experience that helps individuals make new discoveries and recycle discoveries about what they know.

Learning Area 42. Organizing Research Information

Subject Areas: Social Studies/Science/Language Arts/Reading

STUDENTS

1. Search for books, films, filmstrips, and slides relevant to the problem.
2. Gather information, using a scientific procedure of problem solving.
3. Sort information by categorizing and summarizing.
4. Elaborate on the information by discussing, questioning, giving examples, amplifying, and so forth.
5. Retrieve the information by organizing it in a tangible way.

TEACHER

• Helps to develop fact sheets, retrieval charts, and empty booklets for organizing social and scientific study data. Completed data should be displayed at a center for others to study and discuss, along with study references like encyclopedias, almanacs, *Time* magazine, and so forth.

• Develops a guide with the group's help for individuals to follow when organizing research information. With some groups the guide may need to be more detailed than with others.

Learning Area 43. Retrieving Social Studies Data

Subject Areas: Social Studies/Language Arts

STUDENTS

1. Organize people picture books, using drawings or magazine cut-outs:
   Appearances and lifestyles
   Work and play
   Likenesses and differences
2. Keep weekly or monthly calendars of class events and activities for a class history to present to parents and administrators.
3. Prepare fact sheets about people for use in a school newspaper:
   A Fact Sheet on My Grandmother: _____
   Where she lived _____
   Games she played _____
   Chores she did _____
4. Join a small group discussion on socially oriented topics:
   Groups we belong to . . . and why
   Crime and punishment . . . and why
   Poverty and wealth . . . and why
   Prejudice and discrimination
   Leisure time
   Energy limitations
5. Organize a series of illustrated data cards with information on, for example,

Famous women explorers	Wars
Latin American heroes	Parks

6. Design a computer data base of interesting data for a question-and-answer game. Topics might be
   Historical dates
   U.S. states and capitals
   Early cave dwellers
   Native American tribes

TEACHER

• As the students share information learned in a class study, the teacher summarizes it on a large wall chart and then invites individuals and small groups to organize the material on their own and share with the class at a later time.

EXTENDING THE 3 R'S
Learning Areas 44-48

Many times throughout the school day teachers can arrange to extend 3-R's activities into creative, self-selected choices. These activities often can be the "daily requirements" for reading, writing, and arithmetic, replacing the routine type of seatwork that normally follows teacher-directed lessons.

Follow-up activities that call for one answer or for copying material limit the range of understanding that students might otherwise reveal. Assignments and prepared worksheets calling for rote recall or one-answer responses usually rule out the challenge for individuals to take responsibility for organizing their understanding in personally meaningful ways. There is little chance, then, for students to structure and interpret what they have learned so that it can be assimilated.

Activities that are open-ended, on the other hand, allow students not only to show what they have learned but to organize that learning in forms that have personal significance.

Learning Area 44. Reading Activities

Subject Areas: Reading/Language Arts/Social Studies

STUDENTS

1. Use basic stories to
        Prepare duplicated worksheets for others to choose to do
        Organize an illustrated booklet of interesting story sentences
        Organize a dramatic reading or play of the story
        Prepare question-and-answer cards to file
2. Organize a self-paced or self-selected reading program, using basals or library books and keeping records of progress and accomplishment.
3. Read on interest topics in reference books and share the knowledge in a report or other presentation.
4. Study class-made chart stories on
        Plans for a trip or experiment   Discussion standards
        Current events or school happenings   Directions for making
                                                    things

5. Organize a reading club where students may read and discuss stories and poems of interest, prepare choral readings, share original stories, and so forth.
6. Read computer printouts made by students and others, and discuss their meaning.

TEACHER

• Makes available wide reading selections on many reading levels to accommodate individual abilities and interests. Arranges comfortable places for reading with cushions, floor rugs, rockers, lamps, and other inviting settings. Maintains a file of ideas for organizing reading activities and makes table and bulletin board space available for display of original work.
• Provides time to introduce new books and have individuals share books read or reading activities accomplished. Supports individual interests in reading.

Learning Area 45. Reading Activities with Key Words (Self-Selected Vocabulary)

Subject Areas: Reading/Language Arts

STUDENTS

1. Select words from their key-word cards to
      Form sentences on sentence strips and pocket charts
      Use as topics for finding more information to read
      Make an illustrated booklet of words, phrases, or sentences
2. Prepare a story from key word or key phrase cards and put on carbon masters for a class newsletter, or pin up on a flannel board for others to read.
3. Prepare key-word envelopes by writing a story on posterboard, cutting it up into words and phrases, putting these in envelopes, and asking others to pin them up as a rebuilt, unscrambled story.
4. Type key words into a microcomputer and create a graphic illustration by drawing on a KoalaPad Touch Tablet™ (available from Creative Publications).
5. Work with a "talking computer" by typing in a word or sentence while listening to letters and words being typed.

TEACHER

• Confers with individuals regularly to help them to accumulate words important to them and to learn to read and write them in a variety of settings.

• Posts key-word charts on walls, easels, or heavy rings and word ladders, for individuals to use in organizing key-word reading activities, along with their own key-word cards kept in boxes or on rings.

• Studies books such as *Teacher* by Sylvia Ashton-Warner and *Key Words to Reading* by Jeannette Veatch, which have excellent explanations of the process.

Learning Area 46. Spelling Activities

Subject Areas: Language Arts/Spelling

STUDENTS

1. Organize spelling notebooks for misspelled words from personal writing. These can be used for a personal spelling list and studied with a spelling buddy.
2. Make spelling charts of root words, extending them into longer words, rhyming words, contrasting words, multisyllable words, and so forth.
3. List ways to practice spelling words, then organize spelling study groups or a spelling bee for interested classmates.
4. Submit some creative writing to an editorial committee for spelling corrections before publishing in a class newspaper or book.
5. Create spelling games to play on the computer, such as Missing Letters, Scrambled Words, Radar flashed words, and so forth.

TEACHER

• Provides small blackboards, word charts, dictionaries, pocket charts, sentence strips, plastic and cardboard alphabet letters, tape recorders, electronic spellers, and other materials needed to organize spelling practice. Arranges for partner or small-group study and encourages individuals to keep records of their progress.

• In addition to using grade-level spelling lists, stresses basic word lists of the most frequently used words. (Such lists are available in professional books and curriculum guides.)

• From time to time, conducts brief, introductory word-power activities (adding prefixes, suffixes, syllabicating, and so on) with group members paired off at chalkboards. Lists can be developed later into word-pattern charts and posted as resources for individual use.

Learning Area 47. Practicing Math Skills

Subject Areas: Mathematics/Language Arts

STUDENTS

1. Organize worksheets for others to use at a math center, such as
   What is smaller than . . . larger than . . .
   What comes before . . . after . . . between . . .
   What to buy with $10
   Time zones
2. Prepare number cards on posterboard for practice with a partner or small group, in order to master numeral recognition, basic facts, and so on. Results should be graphed.
3. Prepare a scroll or chart of interesting statistics gathered from newspapers, magazines, and record books like the Guinness Book of World Records.
4. Prepare story problems for others to solve with answer key sheets for self-checking. These can be recorded in a Math Practice Book and used for building equations on computers as well as for organizing a flannel-board story or mathematical puppet show.

TEACHER

• Various study centers often offer challenges for integrating math activities with other studies. A fish center might need a chart of water temperatures; a bookmaking center might need book page measurements. Current events areas can also be used daily to draw attention to numbers in the news.

• With the group's help, maintains a math-card activity idea file along with boxes of objects, pictures, and other items for practicing math skills. Boxes might be labeled "Prices," "Sizes," or "Quantities," or they might be used to prepare number charts, graphs, or booklets, according to individual choices and needs.

• Computers and calculators offer endless opportunity for students to organize calculations, problems, equations, and all kinds of graphics for math practice. When individuals are able to organize their practice on electronics machinery, motivation stays high.

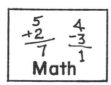

Learning Area 48. Mathematical Projects

Subject Areas: Mathematics/Social Studies/Language Arts/Reading

STUDENTS

1. Organize play-store and business projects:

   Camera shop or gift shop   Supermarket or department store
   Spice or dry goods store   Antique store or supply center
   Shoe shop or toy store   Snack bar or garden center

   Students collect and organize the stock, prepare price tags and labels, inventory books, and keep other number records.
2. Contribute to class number projects:

   Directory of names, addresses, ages, clothing sizes
   Mural of numbers (1,000 pumpkins, fifty Easter eggs), with shapes drawn free-hand, cut out, and mounted on colored paper
3. Help organize a math study center:

   Collect objects and equipment for weighing, counting, sorting
   Collect ideas for working with area, perimeter, or volume
   Prepare number books, worksheets, charts, class logs
   Prepare computer games and disc collections of expert knowledge

TEACHER

• Helps to organize choices of stores or businesses, with students taking responsibility for different jobs. As individuals conduct business or take on consumer roles, the teacher observes and plans discussions of mathematical discoveries as well as emerging problems.

• Keeps the emphasis on problem solving and the social usefulness of numbers.

EXTENDING COMMON EXPERIENCES
Learning Areas 49-54

Common, group-shared experiences frequently can be used to direct individuals toward independent exploration in learning. In following up group experience with opportunities for choices of ways to interpret and organize learning, the teacher deliberately encourages students to think creatively and to use skills that will help them express themselves. As individuals express what they have learned and freely decide upon appropriate forms of expression, they reveal what they have truly understood and absorbed. This gives them a realistic base for satisfaction in achievement and gives the teacher a realistic base for guiding individuals toward deeper knowledge and understanding.

For the spiral to continue, much talk time is called for. Sharing information, discussing ideas, recalling field trips, planning and evaluating cooperatively all take time, but such time for reflection is crucial in extending common experiences into independent activity.

Learning Area 49. Field Trip Follow-up

Subject Areas: Art/Language Arts/Social Studies

STUDENTS

1. Tell about a trip by

    Writing a story   Making a collage picture
    Drawing a story   Making a trip booklet
    Painting or sketching   Making a picture or scaled map
    Preparing a puppet show
2. Organize snapshots or slides into a scrapbook to use in discussion. (These need to be planned in advance of the trip.)

TEACHER

• When groups go on a field trip some of the follow-up activities should be in the form of class discussions and charted summaries of important information gained. At the same time, there are always additional benefits that individuals get from trips, and they should be encouraged to share their personal reactions in ways that seem important to them.

• When individuals go on field trips they can be invited to share their observations in an organized fashion that would be interesting to others.

Learning Area 50. Discussions

Subject Areas: Language Arts/Reading/Social Studies

STUDENTS

1. Share experiences about dreams and fantasies, feelings, or special occasions.
2. Raise questions about current events, books and stories read, or class plans.
3. Take turns contributing and listening to information, opinions, and thoughts on

    Good books to read   Social conditions
    Fables and proverb meanings   The future

4. Suggest new topics and questions for discussion.

TEACHER

• Helps the group decide on interesting topics for circle discussions and arranges comfortable spaces with carpet pads or pillows for small groups who share common interests to get together for conversation.

• Makes sure that discussions are open-ended, with many answers and ideas shared for a lively exchange. Open-ended discussions need some structure, however, and students should be encouraged to organize their thinking by keeping to the subject and listening to each other.

• Prepares, with the group's help, a file of discussion items and a booklet or wall chart of guidelines for carrying on a discussion. Occasionally the teacher may want to provide a tape recorder or portable video for individuals to get feedback on their discussions or help them prepare to share with the class.

Learning Area 51. Listening Activities

Subject Areas: Language Arts/Social Studies/Music

STUDENTS

1. Organize a tape of sounds collected from the classroom, hallways, playground, or street corner. Titles can be given or a story made up to accompany the playback.
2. Listen to a friend or the teacher read aloud a story to talk about, poems to act out, or a book to share.
3. Take turns in small groups listening to classmates tell about

    Scary Things That Happened to Me   What I'm Proud of
    Things I Like and Don't Like to Do   How I'd Feed the World

4. Listen to ethnic and other musical recordings, and organize a musical for group enjoyment.

TEACHER

• Gathers together recordings and tapes, songbooks, storybooks, poetry books, recorders, record players, and slide-tapes. If needed, keeps a file of ideas for what individuals might do to organize activities around their listening experiences, if they wish.

• Reads aloud daily to the group and discusses what might be done with material gathered through listening. Arranges frequent mutual-sharing sessions of results.

Learning Area 52. Large-Scale Projects

Subject Areas: Social Studies/Language Arts

Theodore Lownik Library
Illinois Benedictine College
Lisle, IL 60532

STUDENTS

1. List possibilities for large-group or school projects. These might be
   International Day celebration
   Circus or parade
   Art or science fair
   Assembly or TV show
   Planting flowers or new trees around the school grounds
   Developing a school museum, library, supply center, or computer center
   Working with a senior citizen's nursing home
   Campaigning for school and class officers
   Conducting a litter drive or save-the-seals fundraising campaign
2. Evaluate the feasibility of each project.
3. Help select the final choice.
4. Contribute to the planning and organization.
5. Take responsibility for its completion.

TEACHER

• Encourages meaningful projects that permit students to participate in matters of social concern, as these offer an excellent way to develop school spirit and high morale. They provide a common cause and allow individuals to take on responsibility as well as leadership in organizing the project.

• Suggests specific projects that seem feasible according to the maturity level of the group and, if necessary, serves as project coordinator to ensure completion to everyone's satisfaction.

Learning Area 53. Study Centers

Subject Areas: Social Studies/Language Arts

STUDENTS

1. Set up an investigation center on a topic of interest. Classmates should include specimens, models, instruction pamphlets, information books, reference books, sketch books, charts, and so forth, for others to use.
2. Set up a dramatic play center for studying

    Submarine travel   A clothing store   A TV station
    Hospital life   A space shuttle   A haunted house

    Children can make cardboard constructions, murals, and other props as needed.
3. Set up a make-it center with instructions for making

    Paper flowers, garlands, party favors and decorations
    Refreshment snacks (popcorn, juices, puddings, applesauce, vegetable sticks)
    Books or newspapers, picture frames, greeting cards

4. Set up a skills clinic center, with signups to teach telling time, using the library, riding a skateboard, handling video equipment, working with computers, and so forth.

TEACHER

• Students who have the opportunity to develop study centers not only gain in self-importance but learn to organize their learning in meaningful ways. The teacher needs to provide these opportunities and give whatever assistance is needed.

• The center may be one for the entire school to use and, planned accordingly, designed for placement in the school library, resource center, or a hallway. On the other hand, if intended for a small interest group, it needs only some space in the classroom.

Learning Area 54. Solving Social Problems

Subject Areas: Social Studies/Language Arts

STUDENTS

1. Identify a problem that may involve aspects of classroom life, community needs, or world conditions.
2. Brainstorm the problem to get clear on its dimensions.
3. Propose solutions.
4. Discuss the possibilities for solution.
5. Select a solution to try out.
6. Plan a course of action and help to carry it out.
7. Evaluate the results.

Problems might range from immediate concerns such as how to organize classroom materials or improve a spelling program, to broader ones like caring for the elderly or conserving the environment.

TEACHER

• Helps the group identify a manageable class problem needing a creative solution. Arranges for small groups to come up with proposals or plans to share and discuss, welcoming all efforts and encouraging their development into a plan of action.

• Makes sure everyone realizes how important imaginative and cooperative thinking can be for solving various levels of social problems.

Chapter 5
Independent Activities: Originating

Originating activities push imaginations to the edge of knowledge and beyond. They include new ways of looking at old things, new ways of expressing ideas or feelings, and free experimentations with materials. Through originating activities, individuals learn to express themselves as unique personalities and to appreciate the uniqueness of others. They learn to value the unpredictable and the ambiguous. To do this in a supportive school environment should be every child's right.

In our society of readymade products, prefinished goods, high technology, and urbanized existence, we often find it hard to experience the joy, the invigorating challenge that comes with creating freely. In free creation, we make new things and reshape old things into new forms; we think up new sounds and symbols; we make new discoveries and meet problems in new ways. In the doing, we move toward our potentials as human beings and persons.

In school, where the potential of young people must be nurtured especially, the curriculum should include daily opportunities to work in original ways. Materials centers and open work spaces set up for individuals to serve themselves and find time to create are essential. Understandably, not every kind of self-service center can be available at once. During the year, however, a wide range of choices, carefully planned, should replace most seatwork assignments that focus on conforming, routine, paperwork tasks. Instead of being assigned noncreative seatwork, students can be challenged to use originality in their daily work, and to do so with their own purposes in mind.

Purposes for originating vary according to individual interests, but they also vary in specificity. Sometimes individuals will have a definite objective, intending to create something specific. At other times, they may simply want to try out materials or ideas to see what happens. Either way, children have the right to experience the pleasure of inventive work as part of the school day. Not only do they practice many skills during originating activities, but they gain valuable knowledge—not the least of which is learning to know themselves as originators.

The sampling of originating activities which follows, along with suggestions for teachers, is grouped into four sections: Experimenting with the arts, with thought and language, with technology, and to satisfy curiosities.

EXPERIMENTING WITH THE ARTS
Learning Areas 55-66

The early stages of artistic development involve trying out materials, handling tools, exploring media, and "messing around" with processes. During this time students discover ways to get desirable results. There is no shortcut to this learning. From extended experiences with free manipulation and experimentation children gradually get the feel of artistic expression. They learn what forms a medium can express, how to use a technique or material, how to create a design, how to express an idea through art.

In these early stages of art development, the teacher should promote free experimentation, free manipulation, and free creation, carefully sharing enthusiasm for whatever original results accrue. The results, however, must be the child's, for this is the stuff of creativity, of individuality. To give children a diet of crafts to make, following models and patterns, deprives them of their right to artistic development. Finished-looking, predetermined products made by adult standards, not children's, should be scrupulously avoided. They have no place in a curriculum that promotes creativity.

Children, of course, need to become skilled in procedures, techniques, and safety maintenance, but such skills should accompany artistic exploration, not take the place of it.

Learning Area 55. Experimenting with Art Materials

Subject Area: Art/Science

STUDENTS

1. Try out different ways to paint by using
   Toothbrushes, toothpicks, or fingernails
   Wires, yarns, twigs, or sponges
   Eggshells, cantaloupe rinds, and the like
2. Try different coloring devices on different surfaces:
   Spray painting on boxes, wood strips, pine cones
   Water painting on sidewalks, paper, glass
   Colored dry chalk on wet paper (or vice versa)
3. Experiment with techniques of working with paper and newspaper,
   such as

Pleating	Fringing	Bunching	Curling
Tearing	Braiding	Rolling	Bending
Folding	Scoring	Coiling	Wrinkling
Twisting	Slitting		

4. Experiment with making dyes and paint mixes using
   Natural materials like onion skins or rice grains
   Food coloring drops added to small water jars
   Primary tempera colors

TEACHER

• Discusses open-ended uses of various art materials and brainstorms techniques and materials for experimenting. At times provides a focus for experimenting, such as using a particular material or technique.

• Appreciates the importance of working experimentally with art materials, regardless of how the product turns out. When interesting discoveries are made, encourages their recording and sharing.

Learning Area 56. Forming Paper Designs

Subject Areas: Language Arts/Art

STUDENTS

1. Experiment with paper designs:

> Making triple-layer or open-lattice arrangements by cutting out interesting shapes, repeating the process with several sheets, then stapling on a last sheet for background
>
> Making tissue laminations by cutting designs from colored tissue paper, gluing to wax paper, adding more wax paper, and (between sheets of scrap paper) ironing at low temperature
>
> Weaving paper mats from colored paper or newspaper strips sprayed with enamel paint

2. Design functional pieces such as

> Book jackets or covers for original storybooks
>
> Posters or stamps for a special event
>
> Decorations cut out of fingerpainted or colored paper for bulletin boards

3. Contribute to a large painted or 3-D mural on a special subject such as

A Windy Day	A United World	Yellow is for _____
Halloween	Pioneers	Joy

A mural also can be an abstraction using a squirt-gun or drip painting technique, pastels, or fingerpaints.

TEACHER

• Encourages free art activities that extend beyond a crayon-picture-drawing medium by making available colored construction, tissue, botany, and graph paper; newspaper; cardboard; butcher paper; newsprint; sandpaper; styrofoam; wall, crepe, contact, and corrugated paper; colored paper towels; scraps; roll ends; and colored labeling tape. Also adds: ball point pens, markers, fingerpaints, tempera paints, oil pastels, charcoals, stamp pads, lacquer, glue, and dyed water.

• Allows individuals to practice frequently with the same technique in order to feel satisfied with their efforts. Above all, the stress should be upon the processes of using various design tools, not the end products.

Learning Area 57. Forming Nonpaper Designs

Subject Areas: Art/Social Studies/Math

STUDENTS

1. Create decorative art forms with
        Colored string, wood chips, twigs, buttons
        Styrofoam, plastic pipe cleaners, nylon
        Stained glass, coat hangers
        Twine, grass, weeds, bark
        Macaroni, beads, acorns, yarn
        Tissue, lacquered boxes, cartons
2. Design a structure like a
        Dollhouse or doghouse
        Space walk area with flag designs and symbols for new planets
            and stars
3. Design a handicraft:
        Tapestry or stitchery
        Dried weed or flower bouquet
4. Design a free-form, large sculpture using Lego®, wood blocks, sand,
   or even classmates placed in positions. Unusual results can be photo-
   graphed.
5. Design pictures and shapes for display on a computer screeen. (LOGO
   language makes it easy.)

TEACHER

• Encourages individuals to create their own designs out of unstructured materials, often using old materials in new arrangements.

• All kinds of nonpaper materials can be stored in a classroom if the
teacher provides storage space and labeled boxes. A shelf might be filled
with boxes labeled: seeds, beads, clay, string, wire, paper, packing foam,
cellophane, straw, sand, cotton, plastic wrap, coat hangers, wires, shells,
toothpicks, thin metals, wood strips and scraps, fabric pieces, and other
'junk'.

Learning Area 58. Printmaking

Subject Areas: Art/Science

STUDENTS

1. Experiment with print designs using
   Leaf prints on tile
   Monoprints on tagboard or corrugated cardboard
   Linoleum or cardboard block prints
   Potato prints, carrot prints, or other raw vegetables
   Silhouette, sandpaper, or stencil prints
   Footprints, handprints, elbow and knee prints
   LOGO commands from a computer
2. Form 3-D print arrangements on heavy cardboard with
   Leaves, grass, seeds   Leather bits, old keys
   Twigs and wood scraps   Folded paper, cardboard tubing
   Cloth pieces, moleskin   Cubes or spools
3. Design prints for decorative gift-wrap paper or greeting cards.

TEACHER

• Printmaking is an activity of creative challenge and fun, yet does not call for special art skill. Whether students make simple forms or complex ones will depend upon their level of maturity and the teacher's judgment of what they can handle.

• Provides an art center that includes printmaking materials and space to work on special printmaking projects such as linoleum block printing.

Learning Area 59. Making Art and Craft Patterns

Subject Areas: Art/Social Studies/Technology

STUDENTS

1. Make design or blueprint patterns for construction projects such as furnishings for a playhouse, structures for a model community, and vehicles.
2. Design costume patterns for dolls or for each other.
3. Make patterns for handiwork projects:
   Yarn and paper weaving   Sewing stuffed animals
   Paper or reed baskets   Beaded necklaces
   A class-made quilt   Knitting
4. Create border patterns for stationery, decorative paper, and pages of original stories and books.
5. Create murals of interesting patterns observed on a walk, such as picket fences, railroad tracks, brick walkways, walls, and gardens.
6. Create a procedure for drawing an object or scene on a microcomputer using BASIC or LOGO commands; then demonstrate it to the class.

TEACHER

• Takes the group on walks to look for interesting patterns in the environment, then brainstorms and discusses techniques and useful materials for pattern making on their own.

• Includes in the art center scrap materials such as butcher paper; bits of cloth; scraps of wood, metal, leather, and fake fur; along with tools such as block-print and sewing devices.

• Integrates pattern making with a dramatic play center, such as a stationery store or hat-making factory, where the play activity calls for pattern making.

Learning Area 60. Constructing Mosaics, Collages, and Plaques

Subject Areas: Art/Social Studies

STUDENTS

1. Make a flat collage or hanging using pieces of crayon drawings, torn paper strips, or magazine pictures. These, combined with other textured and colored materials, form a pleasing arrangement that can be glued on oaktag or burlap-covered cardboard.

2. Make a plywood or heavy cardboard plaque using egg carton pieces, buttons, doweling, wallpaper, yarns, trims, and fur pieces. Results can be brushed with India ink for a distinctive effect.
3. Create
>A paper-dot mosaic using colored dots from paper punches
>An eggshell mosaic
>A corrugated-paper mosaic with fabric pieces, cotton, cork, roving, and the like
>A melted-crayon mosaic on aluminum foil

TEACHER

• Invites the group to collect materials for mosaics, collages, and plaques. Labeled boxes might give ideas for what to bring: scraps of colored paper, colored salt, sand, glitter, leaves, dry cereals, feathers, beans, rice, crushed eggshells (dyed various colors), and so forth. These should be made available at an art center where individuals can create designs to satisfy their own ideas. The ideas may be related to current studies or stories that have been read, but this is not necessary. Students often want to create such items in order to make a personal statement or as a reflection of their own personal interests.

Learning Area 61. Creating 3-D Representations

Subject Areas: Art/Language Arts/Social Studies

STUDENTS

1. Create representational paper objects:
   Papier-mâché or clay foods and animals   Tissue-paper flowers
   Paper dolls, costumes, vests, and hats   or kites
                                                     Paper baskets or
                                                        ornaments
2. Make puppets from
   Grocery bags, cardboard tubes, and buttons
   Popsicle or tongue depressor sticks covered with colored crepe
       paper
   Vinyl cloth or nylon stockings
3. Create a small sculpture or object from clay, styrofoam, stovewood scraps, and empty thread spools. This can be used as a prop in telling a story to the class or group of friends.
4. Make shoebox or plywood diorama displays for collections or reports.
5. Mold plaster-relief designs by pouring plaster into a form over objects, then shellacking them for display.

TEACHER

• Three-dimensional representations can be designed for functional purposes or created for personal satisfaction, as individuals choose. In neither case need the productions conform to reality expectations, whether in shape, color, size, or appearance. Originality, not skill in reproduction, should be emphasized, so that students can interpret reality for themselves.

Learning Area 62. Constructing

Subject Areas: Language Arts/Social Studies/Technology/Science

STUDENTS

1. Design and construct large structures:
   Papier mâché world globe   Puppet theater or doghouse
   Junk or snow sculpture   Classroom furniture
   Playground equipment   Cardboard fairy castle or robot
2. Convert the classroom into an environment for dramatic play:
   Space ship or airplane   Submarine ocean travel
   Television studio   Hospital
   Shopping mall   City hall
3. Create and construct small structures:
   Miniature models
   Weaving looms
   Pinhole camera or telegraph set
   Scientific instruments like sundials, wind vanes, rain gauges

TEACHER

• Confers with individuals and groups about plans, materials, and space needed for creating building structures. Monitors their ongoing work, and arranges for older students to assist younger ones, if needed, in solving technical problems that arise.

• Provides space for construction activities inside or outside the classroom and involves everyone in gathering materials: cartons and crates of assorted sizes, wood pieces, lumber, carpenter tools, nails and glue, as well as scrap materials secured from local firms.

• Stresses safety and courtesy guidelines and, if necessary, restricts construction to appropriate times of the day.

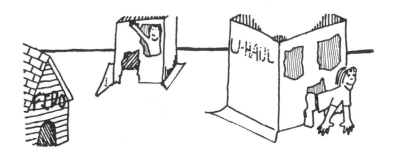

Learning Area 63. Experimenting with Music Making

Subject Areas: Music/Language Arts

STUDENTS

1. Find out which notes on the keyboard combine to make pleasing sounds. Symbol notations can be made up and recorded to show high and low sounds or fast and slow ones.
2. Experiment with different ways to make music with objects such as coconut halves, hands, feet and fingers, and bamboo sticks.
3. Try out different ways to use rhythm instruments in song and musical arrangements. Instruments might be

Shakers	Tambourines	Castanets
Drums	Rhythm sticks	Horns

4. Invent musical sounds for a favorite tale or original story, and tape it for listening center pleasure.

TEACHER

• Views experimenting freely with music making as an artistic experience that should be free of the strain of expectations for making music the "right" way.

• Arranges out-of-the-way space where students can experiment with music making without disturbing others. This may be an outdoor area or a separate, closed-off area away from study areas. The group might even want to try building a soundproof "music studio" as an answer to the noise problem.

• From time to time, musical sharing sessions should be arranged so that students can demonstrate and describe the results of their musical experimentation.

Learning Area 64. Developing Musical Patterns

Subject Areas: Music/Language Arts

STUDENTS

1. Use recordings to develop rhythm patterns for free expression or representation of activities like playing baseball or being wind-blown.
2. Use voices to
> Create chants for class names, interesting words, melodic syllables, and so on
> Add to a favorite melody or convert it to a three-part round
> Put an original tune on a computer that takes musical sounds
3. Use rhythm instruments to create musical patterns or to plan an "orchestral" accompaniment to a well-liked song or piece of music.

TEACHER

• Space in the classroom, hallway area, or outdoors should be set up to give individuals a place to try out their ideas for musical patterns and programs.

• Gathers, with the group's help, an assortment of musical records, tapes, rhythm instruments, and objects to use for music making: clay flowerpots, horseshoes, sticks, brake drums, metal tubes, dangling measuring spoons, shoehorns, glasses, and bottles.

• The teacher also may include charted tagboard or musical sheets for recording patterns. Students can use standard notations, if known, or invent notation systems if they wish.

Learning Area 65. Making Musical Instruments

Subject Areas: Music/Science

STUDENTS

Students make musical instruments that appeal to them by experimenting with materials that make sounds:
> Fishline, wooden boards, and screw eyes (for stringed instruments)
> Pocket combs, pencils, wood blocks, paper cups (for bridges)
> Paper cups, cardboard paint buckets (for resonators)
> Wooden roofing shingles, odd pieces of metal
> Tri-wall cardboard, plastic tubes
> Clothesline, cords, bottle caps, rattling objects
> Large metal containers like tubs or oil cans

Plastic containers, bamboo poles, rhythm sticks, stickers, stones
Shower hoses, water pipes (for horns), tin cans, coconut shells
Milk cartons filled with small objects
Tin pie dishes taped together, filled with small pebbles
Conduit piping (for hanging xylophones)
Bottle tops nailed to small boards

TEACHER

• Gathers, with the group's help, an assortment of materials appropriate for inventive musical instruments and provides a book such as the *Music Instrument Recipe Book* (McGraw-Hill), for students to look through for instrument ideas.

• Completed instruments may be decorated and displayed or stored for use in class rhythm sessions and song fests or small-group musical activity times.

Learning Area 66. Developing Dance Patterns and Movements

Subject Areas: Music/Physical Education/Language Arts

STUDENTS

1. Plan a simple choreography for a dance show, using musical records like "Carnival" or "Peter and the Wolf."
2. Dance freely to a song or record, for enjoyment.
3. Make up gestures and other body movements to accompany story dramatizations. These can be natural, or exaggerated as in a Greek chorus.

TEACHER

• Perhaps the space used for musical exploration also can be used for movement activities. If so, materials like mirrors, musical equipment, record players, records, and costume accessories (scarves, walking sticks, sheets) will heighten the dramatic effect involved in creating self-expressive dance and movement.

• At times, plans a group activity using drums or recordings to invite individuals to create movement and share discoveries. The teacher adds suggestions when appropriate and expresses appreciation for the spontaneous dance patterns and free movements that individuals and small groups have developed.

EXPERIMENTING WITH THOUGHT AND LANGUAGE
Learning Areas 67-71

Language as a symbolic system can be approached playfully, experimentally, and artistically. When we break away from restrictive language and literal expression, we discover the marvelous fluidity of language. We learn that it is changeable, open to interpretation, and very much a part of individual thought and imagination. As we learn to express ourselves in verbal and nonverbal imagery, in analogy and comparison, we extend our abilities to understand and use language more fully, more richly. We extend our range of intelligence, for thinking in metaphorical language taps the resources of intuitive intelligence, a right-brain function that is necessary to the development of wholistic thinking.

Children who have the freedom and encouragement to work inventively and imaginatively with mind and body in the school setting learn to use their intuitive intelligence. They discover the aesthetic aspects of language—its sounds, rhythms, somatic relationships, and artistic imagery. When given opportunities to invent with language and even to "invent" language, using their imaginations, children also learn some of the power and pleasure of both using language creatively and remaining spontaneous and open to new experiences through thought and language.

Learning Area 67. Verbal Imagining and Fantasizing

Subject Areas: Language Arts/Social Studies

STUDENTS

1. Imagine themselves as a certain plant, animal, or machine, brainstorming what they would look like, what they would do, and how they would feel. Ideas can be recorded, dictated, used for writing a story or painting a picture.
2. Take a fantasy trip (directions can be taped), then share with others. Fantasy trips might involve going into a cave to find a treasure, visiting a new world, or whatever. Students also can prepare their own directions to follow.
3. Join a small storytelling group to invent
    Tall tales, absurd questions and answers, or once upon-a-time stories
    Conversations with famous persons of the past
    Episodes for a favorite TV show
    Stories suggested by paintings or other art productions

TEACHER

• Keeps an assortment of literature—fairy tales, myths, legends, fables—in a reading or communications center, for individuals to use on their own.

• Frequently reads aloud to the group and leads fantasy or storytelling sessions, selecting fanciful, high-interest stories. Encourages students to respond spontaneously and with their own "pictures."

• Converses with students who have created art forms, asking questions to evoke details and to stimulate a story plot. Results might be shared with others or put on tape for a listening center.

Learning Area 68. Nonverbal Imagining and Fantasizing

Subject Areas: Social Studies/Art/Language Arts

STUDENTS

1. Create an invention for an exhibit on
       New toys and fashions
       New home-use gadgets
       New machines to solve social problems
       New methods of making life more enjoyable
   These can be sketched with ink, labeled and framed, or made into models.
2. Paint pictures using tempera, water color paints, or felt pens, to use in a storytelling session. Pictures can later be mounted on colored construction paper for display, or made into a picture story book.
3. Contribute to a dramatic play project of invented animals, plants, and environments for a fairy tale, enchanted forest, or science fiction center.
4. Invent pantomimes to illustrate interesting words, phrases, concepts, and ideas.
5. Make a personal coat of arms to share with others. Pictures might include:
       Something you're proud of
       Something you're happy about
       Something nice you did for someone
       Something nice you did for yourself

TEACHER

• Arranges for the collection of fabrics, junk, art supplies, and other materials that might evoke imagination and be useful in nonverbal expression. There should be space not only for display of products but for their use in dramatic play and free conversation.

• Takes the group on camera walks to view the world from unusual perspectives, or plans a fantasy center with the class, as a way of getting started.

• Gives recognition to intuitive intelligence by appreciating spontaneous thinking and encouraging individuals to work nonverbally with their imaginations and fantasies.

• Keeps painting as a daily activity for communicating ideas, both personal and those relating to unit studies. Simple easels or other flat supports to work on, as well as art supplies, need to be on hand. Beginners and others who enjoy art but have limited skill in writing often become ingenious storytellers when free to 'write' through painting.

Learning Area 69. Creating Poetry and Verse

Subject Areas: Language Arts/Reading/Technology

STUDENTS

1. Record free-flowing thoughts about an object or event and share them as an oral reading. If appropriate, the teacher may help to put results in poetic form.
2. Write poems for a personal or class poetry collection. If a computer is available these can be typed in and printed out.
3. Experiment with different poetry, shapes, and forms (haiku, tanka, diamantes) found in various poetry books or suggested by the teacher.
4. Make up a new verse to a favorite song and chart it for a singing session.
5. Type into a computer some alternatives for each line of a cinquain, haiku, or rhymed verse; then try different combinations to make new verse.

TEACHER

• Reads poetry aloud frequently, allowing time for enjoyment of the poems without analyzing them with "recitation" questions.

• Stays alert to opportunities for group verse writing. When an unusual event occurs, such as a bird appearing on the windowsill or flies swarming in the classroom, encourages students to combine their images and thoughts into a group poem. If recorded on paper, it can be reread and enjoyed over a period of time.

• Recognizes certain pieces of free writing as poetry and offers help in converting them to poetic form. Arranges poetry readings for those interested in sharing their poems.

Learning Area 70. Inventing Nonsense

Subject Areas: Language Arts/Reading

STUDENTS

1. Make up a "silly word thesaurus" or other word catalog to add to the library table. It might include silly compounds, puns, idioms, synonyms, and so forth.
2. Make jokes for a joke book or comic strips for a comic book.
3. Create a flow chart to "solve" problems such as
   Fleas on dogs   Angry friends who tattle
   Melting ice cream   Parents who get angry
4. Make up a zany alphabet book or computer printout with pages for
   Silly sentences beginning with same letter
   Words that can be pronounced phonetically but otherwise make
       no sense
   Letters and words not yet existing
   Nonsense metaphors (short as a bug, fat as a house)

TEACHER

• Includes, in a writing or nonsense-writing center, lists of ideas for students to use in creating their own nonsense word projects.

• Welcomes laughter as an important aspect of class life and recognizes the fun involved in being humorous. If the group is interested, helps to plan a "silly" project to share and enjoy.

Mad Monster has one foot bigger than the other. He has big green ears, big blue eyes, a big nose and a big mad frown. He has a tie and a heart from Mad Beauty.

Learning Area 71. Inventing with Numbers

Subject Areas: Mathematics/Language Arts

STUDENTS

1. Create new number systems with a base other than ten, using conventional or original symbols.
2. Suggest shortcuts in arithmetic—easy ways to solve old problems.
3. Fill in wall charts such as "Ten Ways to Make a Gallon" or "New Ways to Measure a Table."
4. Make number puzzles for a puzzle activity file or computer activity.
5. Answer questions in a "What Does It Really Mean to You?" number booklet. Page headings can be such ideas as

   A million   A dollar

   A mile   "33"

TEACHER

• Discusses the importance of working with mathematical language in new and creative ways, helping as needed to devise new combinations, new symbols, and new approaches. Encourages children to go further on their own.

• Also encourages students to develop original materials to add to a math study center that may become a place to test out new equations, new programs, and new number systems and even to work with computers in creative problem solving.

EXPERIMENTING WITH TECHNOLOGY
Learning Areas 72–77

One of technology's latest affordable electronic developments, the computer or microcomputer, brings excitement to the classroom. Even when used for practice work, it becomes an intriguing machine for children to operate. When put in their hands for the purpose of experimentation and discovery, all kinds of creative possibilities emerge.

As students gain control over the machine's operation, they learn to make drawings and designs, prepare graphs, make comparative counts, build mathematical equations, invent games, make spelling puzzles, and compose poems or stories, even music. The process begins with freedom to explore and follow curiosity, perhaps by simply pressing keys on the keyboard. Computers are not delicate instruments; keys and silicon chips don't break. Even young children can learn to program and control computer operation if allowed to communicate with the computer in a natural, easy way and use it as a helpful tool.

As they learn the procedures of input, process, and output, users become aware of the need to work with precise instructional coding. In doing so they face the fallibility of computers, reflected in the maxim that output can be no better than input. Students also get in touch with some of the problems of living with advanced technology and learning to solve them in creative ways, for the benefit of all.

Learning Area 72. Inventing with LOGO Language

Subject Areas: Mathematics/Art/Language Arts

STUDENTS

1. Explore ways to move the turtle.
2. Test out some basic commands such as "forward," "back," "right," "left," and so on.
3. Use commands to design shapes for screen display, such as geometric designs and objects of interest (rock, kite, flower, castle, sunset).
4. Experiment with designs by rotating, spinning, sliding, or repeating.
5. Type in a code for the computer to remember; for example, teach the turtle to remember command sequences in a procedure.
6. Make paper sketches in order to keep a record, or record discoveries in a logbook along with code instructions.
7. Create new LOGO commands for use in programming stories, games, animated cartoons, graphics, and so on.
8. Save and store programs on a disk for reuse.

TEACHER

- Begins with, "Here's the turtle, make it move." If the students get stuck, encourages them to seek answers on their own, suggests using graph paper, drawing, or floor-walking to gain the necessary spatial awareness to correct their own problem or mistakes.
- Stresses that there are many ways to draw a particular design or write a LOGO procedure, and that ideas for using LOGO are all around.
- Makes resources like LOGO disks and *LOGO Discoveries* (Creative Publications) handbook available for individuals to use as idea sources, when working alone and with others.

Learning Area 73. Experimenting with BASIC Language

Subject Areas: Reading/Mathematics/Language Arts

STUDENTS

1. Try keys and observe results.
2. Try out simple commands like PRINT, GO TO, RUN, and so forth.
3. Using BASIC commands, put words in computer to create a short message.
4. Type in a simple design and get computer to print it repeatedly.
5. Run a short program someone else has entered, then try to write a program to duplicate the output.
6. Try to alter a short program by adding or deleting. Start with one-line programs and progress to four or more lines. See which changes are accepted by the computer and which ones prompt error messages.
7. Develop programs using a four-step procedure:
   a. State the purpose of the program, exactly.
   b. Identify variables and formulas by using flowcharts.
   c. Convert the program to the BASIC code.
   d. Enter the program in the computer and run it. If it needs debugging, go back to step b and try again.

TEACHER

- Discusses with individuals what they know about computers and encourages knowledgeable ones to demonstrate to the others. After various individual and group explorations, invites a sharing of discoveries and newly created programs.
- Offers BASIC programming disks, instructional manuals, and paperbacks such as *BASIC Discoveries* (Creative Publications) for individuals to use in experimentation. A video terminal printout machine or teletype should be made available, if possible.

Learning Area 74. Adventuring with Simulations

Subject Areas: Social Studies/Science/Math/Language Arts/Reading

STUDENTS

1. Select software simulation disks to run and then experiment with them. Some open-ended ones include:

Factory	Oregon Trail	Run for the Money
Lemonade	Rocky's Boots	Voyage of Mimi
Rocket Trip	Cross' Aquarium	Tellstar

2. Enter the program from the keyboard, using the right spaces and punctuation.
3. Check out before following the instructions and prompts.
4. Make decisions and check out the consequences as they proceed.
5. Try different solutions.
6. Alter the program in some way, to add to the adventure and outcome possibilities.
7. Write simulation programs for others to enter. This might be a science adventure or experiments with alternative outcomes.

TEACHER

• Arranges for a library of selected software that offers high interaction and lots of decision making, and that allows for modification and extension. Simulations that deal with lifelike situations in simplified "what if" explorations can be particularly challenging and responsive to commands and requests.

• Allows individuals to work together, making collective judgments and decisions, and experimenting with new modes of thought.

Learning Area 75. Computer Gaming

Subject Areas: Reading/Spelling/Mathematics

STUDENTS

1. Think up a game to type in and get others to join in playing.
2. Evaluate the game's effectiveness and revise it as needed before storing it on disk for a class library of computer games.
3. Try out a variety of ready-made software games on disks, to see how they work. These might be

Word games	Detection games
Mathematical games	Fantasy games

4. Experiment with games in books like *BASIC Fun* (Avon Books), adapting parts to use in devising other games.

TEACHER

• Uses as little instruction as possible in helping individuals learn how to program games. If needed, asks older children to help younger ones. Because games have a repetitive quality they can be simple to construct using easy, printed directions. So long as they retain an element of competition, they need not be long or complicated. When they cannot be finished in one setting, unfinished programs can be stored on disk or cassette tape, then brought out to be worked on from time to time.

• Makes sure everyone who wishes has equal opportunity to use the computer. Computer time should not be viewed as reward time or extra work time, but as basic time for experimentation with new technology.

Learning Area 76. Word Processing

Subject Areas: Writing/Reading/Language Arts/Art

STUDENTS

1. Think up a word, sentence, or story to type into the computer.
2. View the story on the screen to see if it's really what was wanted.
3. Work with commands of a word processor disk such as Bank Street Writers program, and correct, edit, and revise to suit. A friend might help.
4. Illustrate a story with LOGO graphic commands or KoalaPad Touch Tablet™.
5. Read the results on screen. If satisfied, make a printout to share with a teacher or friends.
6. If a long story has been developed, it can be made into a book by breaking the story into lines for each page, then drawing an illustration for each page.
7. The printout pages can be bound into a book to read to others, or they may be added to the class library.
8. Create an open-ended story for others to finish or revise, then share endings and revisions with one another.

TEACHER

• Emphasizes story/word content, not its correction. In conference, gets an enjoyable dialogue going on the meaning and experiences behind the words or story.

• Recognizes the difficulty of typing and sometimes conducts touch-typing sessions on a voluntary basis. In the meantime, shows patience for the time it takes some individuals to "type."

• Perhaps makes a card file of word processing commands so students can refer quickly to cards for guidance in making story revisions.

Learning Area 77. Using a Talking Computer

Subject Areas: Language Arts/Art/Reading

STUDENTS

1. Generate language by choosing keys or picture panels and instructing the computer to read aloud the picture, letters, words, phrases, or sentences being typed.
2. Look at the story on the screen and "read" it to make sure it's pleasing, while listening to it being read aloud.
3. Develop repetitive language: Put words, phrases, or sentences in, and have the computer repeat them on the screen many times.
4. Invent patterned phrases or one-line patterned sentences for the computer to repeat.
5. When results seem desirable, have the printer fill a page with the listing. Illustrate the page, if interested, with a KoalaPad Touch Tablet™ before getting the printout.
6. Read other students' prints. These can be made into books, or the disk may be stored for reuse at another time.

TEACHER

• Attaches speech synthesizers to a computer, to make it possible for the computer to "talk" directly to the child at the keyboard. The PEAL system (Programs for Early Acquisition of Language) is one such program worth checking out as a way for children to experience being in charge of their own language development.

• At times, if software is unavailable, the teacher or another knowledgeable person might wish to develop a disk program to make a talking computer a creative possibility for students, especially those having difficulty acquiring language, whether speech, writing, or reading.

EXPLORING TO SATISFY CURIOSITIES
Learning Areas 78–81

With curiosity as our motivator, we poke and pry, ask and try out, test and persist to see what happens. Curiosity starts with freedom to explore for its own sake and leads to efficient learning if we learn what is important to us.

A school environment that is rich with curiosity-arousing materials and situations provides individuals with the place, time, and supplies to explore on their own. As children work on open-ended questions and experiments to satisfy their curiosities, they become originators of new knowledge and new insights. They learn what it is like to be "seekers of truth."

Learning Area 78. Questioning, Quizzing, and Querying

Subject Areas: Language Arts/Reading/Social Studies/Science

STUDENTS

1. Make up questions for group use:
   Opinion questions to investigate a school or local problem
   Factual questions for a study-group quiz board or improvised TV game show
   Thought questions for a question file box
   Unanswerable questions for a "stump-the-expert" game
   Riddles or jokes for a riddle or joke book
2. Create a bulletin board of questions of the day or week, pinning up questions, answers, and illustrations (or answers can be placed on key cards for later sharing).
3. Make lists of questions for personal curiosity searching. Sources can be personal interests, class study topics, or independent observations.
4. Construct questions that are answerable on a computer. Data files of information on various topics can be stored in the computer for retrieval purposes

TEACHER

• Begins studies or follows up field trips by inviting questions and recording them on a large wall chart or master carbon for multiple reference copies.

• Helps students to include different kinds of questions, not only questions of fact and logic, but ones that use imagination, personal judgments, and application. Questions and their answers should be shared in discussions that stimulate individuals and small groups to pose new questions and queries.

Learning Area 79. Experimenting in Science

Subject Areas: Science/Language Arts/Technology

STUDENTS

1. Develop experiments to prove hunches about scientific phenomena:
   - Identify a problem
   - Carry out the experiment
   - Plan an experiment
   - Test and evaluate results
2. Use scientific questions like
   - Why did this fail to work?
   - Is there another way to . . . ?
   - What happens if . . . ?
3. Find ways to
   - Remove salt from seawater
   - Cross-fertilize flowers and plants
   - Demonstrate sun fading and shadowing
   - Illustrate properties of air and water
   - Make a better paper airplane
   - Keep animals warm, fed, and watered over weekends
   - Keep animals from escaping while cages are cleaned
4. Write a computer program for a science experiment and its possible outcomes, or set up a "lab" using software like
   - Atarilab
   - Astronomy Disk
   - Chemical
   - Rocky's Boots
   - Heredity Dog
   - Medical School
   - Dinosaurs

TEACHER

• Allows individuals to follow their curiosities about scientific questions and test them out in their own ways, however crude. Through trial-and-error, discoveries can be made that often lead to further study.

• Includes in the science center a question or problem file of curiosities to explore, and develops ideas for experimentation. Keeps empty-page booklets available for recording and illustrating results, to be used later for discussion and further plans for experimentation.

• Helps to develop the understanding that science is an open-ended process of inquiry, with no end to either the answers or the questions that can be asked.

Learning Area 80. Experimenting with Film Materials

Subject Areas: Language Arts/Art/Technology

STUDENTS

1. Make scratch and doodle films to run on movie projectors, using magic markers, grease pencils, or acetate drawing ink to mark up
   Leader film   Opaque film   Blank film
   Clear film   Discarded film   U film
2. Make slides for viewing centers. To do this,
   Cut heavy, clear, plastic-like visqueen into 2″ × 4″ pieces
   Add material or design to one half
   Fold the second half over the design material
   Insert folded plastic into a slide frame
   Cover the slide with several layers of newspaper
   Press it with a warm iron to seal the plastic and frame
Students can experiment with varied materials such as crayon chips, food coloring, cotton thread, grains, moss, crystals, and so on.

TEACHER

• Helps the group plan a class project such as making a scratch-and-doodle film. For this, uses a roll of 16-mm film long enough for everyone to have one or two frames to work with. Discusses techniques for scratching images on the emulsion side with scissors, x-acto knife (requires small-muscle control), pins, hairpins, or stylus. Also discusses film technicalities, such as the purpose of sprocket holes and the relation of projector speed to film frames. After the class shares the film, the teacher sets out materials for individuals or small groups to try ideas on their own.

• Arranges time, space, and materials with which students may experiment and make interesting discoveries.

Learning Area 81. Experimenting with Cameras and Audiovisual Media

Subject Areas: Language Arts/Technology/Art

STUDENTS

1. Improvise a one-minute, nonlinear video collage taking different kinds of shots of shadows, dance snatches, faces, objects from unusual angles, and so forth. Captions can be prepared if the collage is to be shared.
2. Experiment with making a short, unrehearsed, self-portrait videotape with the help of a partner, then play back and monitor on a small camera screen.
3. Shoot a cartridge of movie or still film, exploring photographic elements like angles, position, speed, and movement. Discoveries can be shared in a small camera club.
4. Make illustrations for opaque projector viewing to accompany an original, taped poem or story.

TEACHER

• Equipment like tape recorders and opaque, slide, and film projectors should be generally available, and students should be trained to handle them. Other equipment such as a videotape camera and monitoring screen can often be borrowed. Videotape has the advantage of being reusable, in contrast to slide and print film, which can be used only once. In any case, the equipment and materials should be used for artistic purposes, with individuals and small groups free to use them inventively.

• Takes the class on a camera walk (either movie or video camera), letting everyone take a shot or two. Discussion and supervised film processing or playback can focus on technical aspects of working with cameras.

• Camera work can be part of a communications or other study center when appropriate. If there is a camera center, with a darkroom for processing film, the teacher might arrange for a camera buff (perhaps an older student or aide) to supervise the area until others are accustomed to handling film development themselves.

Chapter 6
Independent Activities: Communicating

Communicating activities involve sharing what has been done, explaining things, discussing ideas, raising questions, solving problems, and using reading and writing to assist thinking. In this sense, communication functions as part of all independent activity work. Individuals whose goals are to search, organize, and originate find themselves communicating informally and functionally, as a means to their ends.

Yet communicating activities, at times, serve a different end, becoming themselves the purpose of work. Sometimes students get started in searching, organizing, or originating with the full intention of producing a presentation, performance, or product to be shared with others. Here audiences are needed: listeners, readers, observers/recipients of whatever the presenters, performers, writers, actors, or speakers have to offer. In a productive atmosphere where activities for independent work abound, all group members will have their turns being receivers as well as givers of creative efforts.

Communication depends upon a number of factors: (1) having something to express and share; (2) feeling a need to do so; (3) being able to express and share using appropriate symbols; (4) having freedom to express and share; and (5) being committed to a give-and-take, reciprocal relationship of open exchange. When these conditions are fulfilled, communication functions as a creative process that enhances the life of everyone involved.

To achieve creative communicating in the classroom requires that group members become communicators; that is, that they share regularly with one another. Talking, writing, reading their writing, listening, performing, presenting, discussing, and engaging in other communication forms take time. Teachers help by reducing their own talk time and increasing opportunity for student talk time among peers. Individuals who work cooperatively in searching, organizing, and originating learn to listen to one another in a natural communication setting. They learn the importance of speaking up and sharing their creative thinking with others.

To expedite this, the teacher and group can designate common work areas and table space for informal exchange, and they can arrange space and time for more formal presentations and performances. When the purpose for creative, independent activity includes deliberate intention to share results with others, communication skills are practiced in a meaningful learning environment, as useful tools for enhancement of self and others.

As individuals perform and share, the teacher gets basic clues for individual and group growth needs, as well as indicators of progress made. These observed clues and indicators usually show far better where children are in their true development of communication skill than do the usually-entrusted activities of testing and assigning out-of-context "language" seatwork exercises.

The sampling of communicating activities and suggestions for teachers that follows is divided into six groupings: writing with art, writing messages, preparing bulletin boards, writing books, using interest centers, and producing movies and plays.

WRITING WITH ART
Learning Areas 82-85

There are many ways to express ideas, present messages, and tell stories. Using art is one way, accomplished through the art form itself, through oral explanation, or, often, with some writing. The importance of writing for communication purposes seems obvious; but equally important is the use of art. Although pencils or pens are widely used for writing, they cannot substitute for the sweep of thoughts and feelings permitted with paintbrush or other art tools. When the brush and pencil are combined, art and writing work together effectively.

In the classroom, writing with art allows children to communicate as individuals who have something important to record in images as well as in print. The content of their offerings can be a reflection of personal interests or acceptance of individual responsibility in relation to a group undertaking. Either way, the integration of writing and art provides practice both in artistic expression and writing skills. What is spelling practice for, if not to permit self expression in written communication? Why work with correct sentence sense if not for use in communicating? Without the need for recording thoughts, who needs to practice handwriting?

When individuals write and paint as part of daily curriculum their talents as authors-artists-in-communication are nurtured.

Learning Area 82. Book Sharing Through Art

Subject Areas: Reading/Art/Language Arts

STUDENTS

1. Make book jackets of favorite books to hang up as a large wall display in the library.
2. Give a "sketch-it-on-the-overhead-projector" chalk talk about a book that is recommended to others.
3. Choose an art form to use in giving a book report:

Scroll   Collages   Drawings

Posters   Maps   Computer graphics

TEACHER

• Leads book-sharing circles for the class, when individuals tell about books recently read, using their art productions to enhance the telling.

• Uses a reading or art center to maintain a file of book-sharing ideas.

• Conducts reading conferences with individuals and small groups to help them plan to share their reading in artistic ways.

Learning Area 83. Slide and Filmstrip Writing

Subject Areas: Social Studies/Language Arts/Art/Technology

STUDENTS

1. Prepare to tell a slide-show story. Slides can be made from
   Cellophane, plastic wrap, wax paper
   Scotch tape, tracing paper, acetate paper, plexiglass
   Filmstrip material—discarded slides, negatives, filmstrips, U-film
   (opaque filmstrip material)
   Snapshots taken on field trips
   Figures and scenes can be made with crystallizing paint or glass paint
   dropped on with an eyedropper.
2. Make a silent filmstrip story for a viewing center. Illustrations can be
   traced onto 35mm film (using special colored pens and splicing the
   film before adding script lines to each filmstrip). The result can be run
   through a regular filmstrip projector for enjoyable viewing.

TEACHER

   • Slides and filmstrips, made without camera equipment and materials, can be done simply and quickly without complicated techniques.
They can be drawn on paper to be used in improvised projectors, or
developed on plexiglass and clear leader film for viewing through real
projectors. If the latter, the teacher shows how imprints can be made
with grease pencils, crayons, and crystal paints or by using an x-acto knife
to scratch out pictures.

Learning Area 84. Making a Picture Storyboard

Subject Areas: Language Arts/Reading/Social Studies

STUDENTS

1. Select an action scene. Make two copies, one to be cut into parts and the other for the final frame.
2. Slide a cardboard frame over the picture to identify interesting sections that could be used in creating a story or message.
3. Cut out selected portions into identical squares and arrange in a progression of frames.
4. Caption the storyboard and paste the frames on a heavy cardboard strip or long roll of paper for viewing on an opaque projector.

TEACHER

• Discusses the possibility of a storyboard project in relation to a class study topic. Explains its procedure and helps small groups find appropriate pictures and images, learn to scrutinize picture details for unusual relationships, and practice sequencing images to create a message.

• Keeps a file of study prints, action photographs, and picture magazines like *Life* and *National Geographic* (dual copies if possible), along with cardboard or cardboard frames for individuals to use in preparing their own storyboards. Storyboards can be used to communicate facts, express feelings, recreate a memory, or make a personal statement about a concept like love or democracy.

Learning Area 85. Book and Magazine Publishing

Subject Areas: Language Arts/Reading/Social Studies

STUDENTS

In developing a book or booklet for publication:

1. Decide what to write about
2. Prepare a draft
3. Edit and revise
4. Plan illustrations, comic strips and cartoons, if any are to be used
5. Design sample book pages
6. Print final version
7. Illustrate, using mounting press
8. Bind, cover

TEACHER

• Gives students the responsibility for turning their own original work into "published" writing. Depending upon individual interests and abilities, certain materials would be appropriate:

    Construction, contact, or laminating paper
    Thin or thick cardboard
    Crayons and watercolors, block and inking sets
    Calligraphy pens, stylus pens, lettering pens, stencils, felt pens
    Duplicator, mimeograph machine, offset machine (or access to one), printing press
    Boxes of cloth, wallpaper, braid, yarn, leather
    Sewing machine and materials for hand sewing (needles, awl, thread)
    Typewriters, drymount press, laminating machine or iron
    Stencils, duplicator carbon paper, botany paper
    Paper cutter, paper punch, glues, binding tapes

• Provides magazines like *Ranger Rick* and the *Electric Company* as models for creating a school or class magazine for enjoyment and use.

WRITING MESSAGES
Learning Areas 86–89

When writing messages, we generally know why we are writing and we usually have someone or some group in mind as recipient of the message. Often we want a message in return, which sets up a give-and-take system of writing.

Since messages are usually concise and to the point, they offer success to those who are struggling to master writing skills. In writing messages, individuals practice skills like following letter forms, sequencing, addressing envelopes, capitalizing, spelling, and punctuating. Even more, they recognize writing as basic, ongoing communication.

Learning Area 86. Writing Letters and Notes

Subject Areas: Language Arts/Social Studies/Spelling

STUDENTS

1. Write personal letters to relatives or friends, which can include thank-you notes, what's-happening letters, and cheer-up letters.
2. Write civic-minded letters to
   The local or school newspaper editor
   Community leaders or congresspeople
3. Write business letters to request information or materials or to show appreciation for a service.
4. Write pen-pal letters to exchange cultural information. These can be collected into a book of letters for all to read and enjoy.
5. Write fun messages to share with others:
   Happygrams   Secret coded notes
   Dear Abby letters   Rhebus letters
6. Prepare petitions for world peace, animal life, clean air, or whatever seems urgent in current affairs.

TEACHER

• Motivation for real letter writing generally is high and the teacher needs only to tap this interest. If needed, offers help by taking dictation and guiding the use of appropriate letter forms.

• A classroom post office center can serve as a useful source of letter writing. Letters to classmates can be mailed, processed, and distributed by children serving as sorters and letter carriers.

Learning Area 87. Making Cards

Subject Areas: Language Arts/Art

STUDENTS

1. Make holiday or get-well cards to send to friends and others.
2. Contribute to a large class birthday card for a classmate.
3. Prepare greeting cards using stenciled wood blocks and ink pads, to put in a greeting card center or "card shop" for dramatic play.
4. Recycle old cards for a card-making center. Outside covers can be used with new inside thoughts, or the cover figures and scenes cut out and pasted on new cards.

TEACHER

• Encourages individuals and small groups to make cards for special occasions and for special people whenever it seems appropriate. Shares designing techniques and ways to use parts of old cards in new designs.

• Plans with the group to establish a card center or store where cards can be made and sold. Stamp pads, a cardmaster duplicator, print sets, and other materials for creating and duplicating cards are useful items in building up the store's inventory. Ample time should be allowed for individuals and small groups to use the card shops in dramatic play.

Learning Area 88. Writing at Home

Subject Areas: Language Arts/Reading

STUDENTS

1. Write at home about life events, thoughts, ideals, feelings and emotions, ambitions, and so forth. Bring some of this writing to school.
2. Write a line story on a home computer, then illustrate it and obtain a printout to read.
3. Make books of "at home" writing and prepare to share them with the class.

TEACHER

• As soon as students write a little on their own, they should be encouraged to bring the results of their home writing to school. To expedite this, the teacher provides a packet of ten to twelve sheets of newsprint for each child to take home. A list of topics brainstormed with the individual or class can also be included, to help parents get the student started.

• Stories brought in are placed in a box containing a folder for each student, arranged alphabetically. When ten or more stories accumulate in a folder, the student can make them into a book and read a few of the stories to the class before putting the book in a reading center for others to enjoy.

• Where home computers exist, students have the opportunity to compare stories using a keyboard instead of handwriting process. At times the whole class might be invited to visit the home and view a demonstration.

Learning Area 89. Notices and Announcements

Subject Areas: Social Studies/Language Arts

STUDENTS

1. Answer a class need (posted by the teacher or a committee), such as needing someone to invent or design

    A game to help in practicing   A computer game to help in
        addition facts   learning new words
    A way of keeping track of   A guest book for visitors to sign
        scissors
    A way to handle a fire drill
2. Make a personal or committee request, such as
    I need five children for a play   Who will listen to our story?
3. Read and share plans, such as
    We will see a film today (from the teacher)
    I have a record to play today (from Sue)
    See Danny's tadpoles
    Computer Club will demonstrate new LOGO color designs at 1:00
4. Print and read reminders, such as
    Tomorrow is Bank Day   Lunch today is _____
5. Post and sign a personal news item, such as
    We have a new baby sister. (Joe)
    A submarine crossed under the North Pole. (Kim)
    My new dog's name is Gus. (David)

TEACHER

• Reserves bulletin board space for all kinds of items to be posted by the teacher and group members.

• Notices may be prepared on posterboard strips and charts may be put up for individuals to use in volunteering for special responsibilities or information called for. To keep the board orderly, sections can be lined out with strips of colored paper or string, and students can take charge of keeping the board up to date.

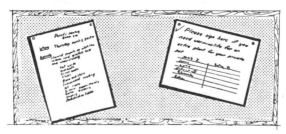

PREPARING BULLETIN BOARDS
Learning Areas 90-92

Bulletin board displays prepared by individuals and groups serve a variety of communicative purposes. They can be used to present study results, to share individual and group interests or concerns, to give space to post notices and announcements, to give special recognition to one another, and even to share results of skills practice efforts.

Children who have frequent opportunity to create school and classroom bulletin boards learn to plan, organize, and create communications in aesthetically appealing ways. They learn the value of artistic, visual presentations of messages. To make sure this happens, teachers need to allow individuals and groups to prepare bulletin boards for their own communicative purposes. Teachers must resist the traditional temptation to "put up" the bulletin boards, because learners will miss out on opportunities not only to solve problems and work creatively but also to learn shared responsibility for the school and classroom environment.

In preparing bulletin board displays, students deal with communication problems beyond speaking and writing. They practice many art skills: selecting pleasing color combinations; observing proportion and spacing, creating shapes and forms from imagination; combining paper of assorted shapes, colors, and textures; and drawing and painting freely, with strong strokes on large paper. Language skills, too, are involved: choosing the main idea, choosing a few words to convey a broad meaning, making meaningful captions, using color and design to carry a message, and emphasizing ideas by color choices and letter sizes. These and other related skills are not developed in sentence and paragraph exercises but in individual and group problem-solving activities that put communication skills to the real test.

Learning Area 90. Personal Recognition Bulletin Boards

Subject Areas: Social Studies/Language Arts

STUDENTS

1. Try for a selected display of
   "Artist of the Day"
   "Story of the Day"
   "Original Arithmetic Problems"
2. Take turns selecting and pinning up original work for "My Display," with everyone responsible for a day's display.

3. Take turns being the class celebrity for a class graffiti. Students pin up snapshots of themselves, while class members write comments and make illustrations with colored pencils or felt pens, to

     Tell positive attributes and behaviors about the celebrity

     Note special skills or talents

The group should read the completed graffiti aloud to the celebrity.

4. Contribute newsworthy items for a bulletin board on

     "We Are Proud of Ourselves"   "We Work Well Together"

     "Our Computer Discoveries"   "Our Efforts for Peace"

Class members describe their contributions, achievements, and efforts and pin up the results.

TEACHER

• Takes charge with a small committee for bulletin-board displays of special recognition. For this, students submit their products to the committee or teacher for selection, based on well-understood criteria.

• Displays and committees should be changed frequently and the types of displayed work varied, to give recognition to everyone's talents.

Learning Area 91. Personal Information Bulletin Boards

Subject Areas: Language Arts/Social Studies/Science

STUDENTS

1. Share vital statistics for a bulletin board, as
      Where do you live? (Draw your house and street and write in your
         address.)
      Who are you? (Make a self-portrait and write your full name.)
      Who is your family? (Make a family portrait and write in
         members' names.)
      What is your trip to school? (Draw a map showing your route to
         school.)
2. Draw and cut out pin-ups that represent personal interests, such as
      Things I Like to Do   Places to Play
      Favorite Books   Favorite Animals
      My Idea of Kindness   Things I Want to Learn About
3. Search for baby pictures and other snapshots of self and family for a
   bulletin board display.
4. Brainstorm with a group or partner to make long action lists to pin up
   on a bulletin board. Starters might be
      I used to be ＿＿ but now I ＿＿   I am ＿＿
      I choose ＿＿   I can ＿＿

These can be selected, illustrated, and organized into an "I Have
Power" display.

TEACHER

    • Uses bulletin boards, with inviting captions and questions, to draw
out information of a personal nature. Students can paint, draw, or cut out
illustrations and write information for the display.
    • Also makes available small flannelboards, corkboards, chipboard
or heavy cardboard pieces for individual and small-group bulletin board
making. Assists in editing and arranging materials, as needed.
    • Provides daily opportunities for students to share their produc-
tions, feelings, and preferences, with a sense of pride and self-apprecia-
tion.
    • Conducts discussions that permit individuals to share orally in an
accepting, nonjudgmental environment. Encourages bulletin board sharing as a way to further mutual appreciation of one another.

Learning Area 92. Using "Research" Bulletin Boards

Subject Areas: Social Studies/Language Arts/Science

STUDENTS

Contribute to a study group's questions posted on a research bulletin board, then

1. Look in books or interview people to find answers.
2. Prepare short descriptions and illustrations to place on the bulletin board as answers.
3. Study the bulletin board to find what others have found out about the topic.
4. Suggest new questions to be placed on the bulletin board.
5. When it is time to change the bulletin board, some children might use the information for a book to be placed in the library.

TEACHER

• Provides small bulletin boards for individual and small-group use. Also, arranges opportunities for discussion of the answers.

• Class bulletin-board space also can be reserved for individuals to use in sharing results of their research on topics of class interest.

• Many topics of current interest for bulletin board displays emerge from class discussions. After a topic of interest is chosen and researched, students can be encouraged to paint or draw and cut out their creations, sometimes writing or dictating titles to accompany them, sometimes working at the computer. When the contributions are ready, the teacher works with the class or a committee to arrange the display in an attractive and meaningful manner.

WRITING BOOKS
Learning Areas 93–100

Self-confidence in communicating ideas grows when individuals see results in a tangible form, such as a book. They see their writing in totality, with each page having its own meaning yet relating to "something bigger." This brings about a feeling of adequacy in communication that cannot be obtained from doing a worksheet for practice and correction. To do a paper "because the teacher says so" has little potential for building confidence in expression of personal ideas. Writing books is an accomplishment, an expression of individuality.

Books may be dictated by the youngest children, but older ones should learn the skills needed to develop their own projects over a long period of time. Produced in an assortment of shapes and kinds, books can be carefully drafted and bound or simply done as stapled booklets. Whatever the form, book writing gives real reasons for practicing basic language skills, such as

Writing neatly and legibly
Organizing ideas in sequential patterns
Using correct word meanings and newly acquired words
Using clear sentence structure and correct grammar
Understanding that books are written to serve many purposes.

In addition to the development of personal skills in organizing and expressing ideas, bookmaking stimulates a deeper appreciation for books that other people have written. It is one of the steppingstones to a lifetime enjoyment of reading and writing.

Learning Area 93. Making Class-Story and Literary Books

Subject Areas: Language Arts/Social Studies/Reading

STUDENTS

1. Compose story books, such as
     Humorous Stories   Just-So Stories   Fables
     Tall Tales   True Tales   Riddles and Jokes
2. Make scrapbooks of favorite stories, poems, or songs for a class anthology.

3. Draw pictures for a group-planned wordless picture book.
4. Make an extended story or comic strip, with everyone who wishes contributing a sentence, paragraph, or page. Sometimes this can be done on a computer, when available, with different versions listed and used in new combinations.
5. Make a touch-and-feel book, using small, lightweight objects and fabric pieces glued on pages, with questions or descriptions added.

TEACHER

• Promotes the development of storybooks, whatever the student's age. At first, assumes responsibility for taking dictation and recording stories to accompany pictures. As individuals mature, they write their own pages, and the teacher simply helps to organize materials, provide time, and recognize the work done.

• Uses a publisher's center as a place to stock necessary materials and equipment for producing books. Students who are advanced in their writing should be expected to work with a sense of care and high standards.

Learning Area 94. Making Topical Scrapbooks

Subject Areas: Language Arts/Reading/Social Studies/Science

STUDENTS

1. Work on holiday themes, such as

Halloween fun	Valentine designs	Cinco de Mayo
Christmas joy	Easter bonnets	Lunar New Year
Chanukah customs		

2. Use general topics, such as

Science is everywhere	Insects	People we know
Winter here and there	Air	Best friends

3. Make category picture books, such as
     Dogs: pet dogs, show dogs, wild dogs
     Tools: hand tools, power tools, levers, pulleys
     Vertebrates: mammals, reptiles, fish, birds, amphibians
     Airplanes: airplanes of long ago, modern airplanes, future ones
     Seasons: seasons in the hemispheres, equator regions, far north and far south

TEACHER

• Uses picture and word scrapbooks of various kinds as an easy-to-do independent activity for individuals and small groups, and sometimes prepares the scrapbook forms: stapled books, cut-and-fold tagboard strips for accordion-type books, or perforated black construction paper sheets for album-type books. Students then can make their own cover titles and designs.

• As a starter, prepares a large blank book with titled pages to be filled in, or simply collects pages made and assembles them. These can be used as "big books" for beginning reading activities. Pictures for scrapbooks can be drawn, painted, or cut out, and captioned or labeled.

Learning Area 95. Making Personal Books

Subject Areas: Social Studies/Language Arts

STUDENTS

1. Make an "All About Me" or "This is My Life" book with drawings or snapshots:

Wishes	Friends	Babyhood	Pets
Future	Hobbies	Family	Travel

2. Make fill-in booklets using sentence beginnings like

   If I could be . . . , then I would be (or have). . . .
   I am . . . I am not . . . (or can and cannot).
   I like . . . I don't like . . . (or want and don't want).
   I used to . . . but now. . . .

3. Select a self-topic as a book theme:

I Like to Eat	I Get Glad When
I Get Mad When	I Get Scared When
I Like to Play	My Favorite Sports

4. Contribute to a "What Does it Mean to You?" booklet. Page headings might be

A million	Freedom
A dollar	USA
Peace	Family

5. Make an illustrated alphabet book or dictionary on topics of personal interest and expertise.

TEACHER

• Because the information for these books comes from the individual's life experiences, it requires no special research. The teacher needs merely to encourage this kind of communication and to respect the authenticity of its contents. Word books such as these not only promote precision of thought and vocabulary expansion, but also have the advantage of promoting early success in bookmaking. The books are easy to make, yet they give reading and writing practice, along with creative artwork opportunities.

• Keeps a file of sentence beginnings or a dummy book of such beginnings, for individuals to use as prototypes for their own, if they wish.

Learning Area 96. Making Fact and Information Books

Subject Areas: Social Studies/Science/Language Arts

STUDENTS

1. Prepare a class directory of names, addresses, telephone numbers, and services and resources available.
2. Prepare a source book on
     Good places to eat   Interesting places in town to visit
     Rainy day games   Saturday fun
3. Write a nonfiction book on a topic of personal expertise for the library:
     Being an artist   Animals of the nearby woods
     Making friends   Living around the world as a military child
4. Contribute to a school almanac
     Principals and teachers, past and present   Famous graduates
     School origin and history   Geographical layout
5. Compile a school or class *Guinness Book of World Records* including
     Who traveled the farthest   Who has the most siblings
     Youngest and oldest   Who has attended the most schools

TEACHER

• Some individuals prefer making documentary or statistical kinds of books, rather than storybooks. These books usually are serviceable and fun to make, whether done simply, with a few pages of information, or elaborately.

• A book center should include invitations to prepare information books: almanacs, directories, encyclopedias, record books, and so forth. Individuals gather information through interviews and research, or use their own background of knowledge.

Learning Area 97. Writing Fiction

Subject Areas: Language Arts/Art/Reading

STUDENTS

Those interested in writing and "publishing" fiction join a writers' workshop to

1. Discuss sources of writing, such as personal experiences, observations, and imagination.
2. Decide what to write about—anything from a fairytale to a sports adventure.
3. Outline a "plot" or sketch out a story.
4. Begin to write a story, chapter by chapter, or section by section. Spend time getting ideas just right.
5. Request criticism and suggestions from classmates by forming editorial groups of two or more.
6. Have conferences with the teacher before writing a final draft.
7. Prepare a dummy book copy, laying out the final draft page by page.
8. Print or type out the manuscript.
9. Add illustrations or arrange for an illustrator from among classmates.
10. Use a dry-mount press for illustrations, prepare the book form, and have a shoemaker sew the binding (or use another method of binding).
11. Read the "published" book to other authors or an appreciative audience, before perhaps contributing to a "school authors" library or book sale.

TEACHER

• Takes a group through the process by developing a group-made fiction book. Helps the group decide on a story outline, and works with the group to develop the story. Delegates the writing and artistic responsibilities, as well as the printing.

• The completed book may be presented to a children's hospital or to young children, if appropriate. Individuals and small groups might then write their own fiction books, if interested.

Learning Area 98. Making How-to Books

Subject Areas: Social Studies/Language Arts

STUDENTS

1. Prepare a guidebook to help others learn a skill or art:
       How to Ski (Bicycle, Play Soccer)
       How to Clean Houses, Yards, Garages
       How to Care for Pets
       How to Program a Computer
       How to Camp Out
       How to be a Welcomed Guest
       How to Babysit (or do other jobs)
2. Develop a how-to manual for others to use in construction:
       How to Make a Dollhouse   How to Make a Submarine
                                                         Sandwich
3. Write an illustrated book explaining how to use:
       Cooking and baking utensils   Playground equipment
       Tools (carpenter's, mechanic's,   Cameras
            boater's, gardener's)   Computers

TEACHER

• As areas of expertise surface among group members, the teacher proposes a project of making how-to books. Invites those who are interested in writing a how-to book to a writers' meeting to discuss the art and science of such a production. Shows samples for discussion and serves as consultant throughout the manuscript production.

• When done, students may wish to prepare how-to centers by arranging table displays of their books, needed equipment and materials, using these to give demonstrations.

Learning Area 99. Making Math Books

Subject Areas: Math/Language Arts/Social Studies

STUDENTS

1. Develop an individual book of original problems or contribute a page to a class-made math book.
2. Make a book of arithmetic games and puzzles for others to enjoy.

3. Make personal number books about classmates for sharing
   Birthdays and times between them
   Distances traveled between school and home
   Comparisons of heights, weights, and clothing sizes
   Allowances and how they are spent
4. Make mathematical scrapbooks using magazine collections or free drawings:

Math in the daily news	A baseball book of numbers
Geometric shapes	A week's grocery costs
Number patterns	Fractional equivalence

5. Prepare an instruction book for writing a computer program of mathematical problems. Books can contain various mathematical problems that have been developed and printed.

TEACHER

• Math books are a useful way to communicate mathematical knowledge. Not only do students organize mathematical symbols, they learn about their importance in everyday living and how to communicate through numbers.

• Stimulates the group to observe quantitative aspects of living and to express observations in book form. This expression often gives clues to individual levels of understanding, which can be used in preparing small-group and individual instruction or skills practice.

Learning Area 100. Making Phonics and Grammar Study Booklets

Subject Areas: Reading/Spelling/Language Arts

STUDENTS

1. Make illustrated phonics booklets of words found in readers and other books. Pages can be devoted to words that
   End in "ing"   Have long or short vowels
   Can be contracted   Start with blends
2. Make a grammar stripbook of words or sentences, divided up by categories:
   Connectors and phrases   Subject and predicate
   Things and places   Actions and describers
   Singular and plural   Idioms and slang
3. Make a book of extended sentences, starting each with a simple subject and predicate and rewriting it several times, each time making it more elaborate, with modifying words, phrases, and clauses. This can be done on a computer and printed out, if a computer is available.
4. Make a phonics, spelling, or grammar workbook for others to do. (Pages should be covered with plastic so grease pencils can be used, permitting work to be erased.)
5. Prepare a glossary for an original book or other stories.

TEACHER

• Keeps opportunities open for language study. Starts by using bulletin board space with captions or by placing blank books in the room with titles for grammar and language analysis.

• Suggests, during reading and spelling conferences, that individuals make phonics or word-structure booklets when needed to reinforce word recognition and spelling power. These study books can be used for the children to practice alone or in small groups.

I Can Be.....
written and illustrated by
Karla Curry

I can be your friend
until the very end
page 5

USING INTEREST CENTERS
Learning Areas 101-104

Children need to communicate in many ways and on many topics. Large-group oral sharing gives some opportunity for this expression, but much more can be accomplished at interest centers, special places where peers communicate freely with one another. Here they use a variety of communication processes and practice a host of social skills. They learn not only to exchange ideas openly but to work cooperatively, preparing written and oral productions for sharing. Interest centers also serve as places where individuals invite others to participate in enjoying good stories, exchanging messages, constructing picture stories, or adding to a storybook for class enjoyment.

Some classrooms have only a few centers, which are changed frequently; others have a larger number, which function over a longer period of time. Sometimes corners do the trick; sometimes corridors, coat closets, outdoor areas or any out-of-the-way space will do so long as classmates can work together on a common interest. The group should participate in the setting up of some centers, taking over not only their care and maintenance but their development. The teacher's task, then, is to help find space and materials and to insist that participants be responsible for the centers. There can be many kinds of interest centers, limited only by the group's imagination.

At interest centers individuals choose and develop activities at their own level of ability, thereby accommodating their own individual differences.

Learning Area 101. Magazine and Newspaper Center

Subject Areas: Language Arts/Social Studies/Art

STUDENTS

1. Examine magazines and newspapers for ideas about types of stories, games, articles, columns (Dear Abby letters, editorials), illustrations, and so forth.
2. Make contributions voluntarily or on assignment from the editorial committee.
3. Work on a proofreading or editorial committee to get material ready for the printer or typist. Or, use a computer word processor procedure.
4. Cut stencils of illustrations.
5. Assemble the newspaper or magazine.
6. Make attractive covers for class magazines.

TEACHER

• Students enjoy reading and doing the activities in such standard magazines as *Highlights for Children, Weekly Reader,* and *Junior Scholastic,* or newer ones like *Ranger Rick* and the *Electric Company.* They also enjoy creating their own newspapers and magazines. If the teacher provides a few samples, plans for time for writing and publishing, and provides space for an office, the group will do the rest.

• A class newspaper may start with dictation to the teacher, but even then the responsibility for make-up, news gathering, editing, and publishing should be the group's. Students, on their own, write or sketch for the proposed publication. An editorial staff designates where to receive contributions and from time to time suggests, with the teacher's help, which sections need additional material.

Learning Area 102. Performance and Demonstration Corner

Subject Areas: Language Arts/Math/Social Studies/Art/Science

STUDENTS

1. Put on a rehearsed play or poem interpretation. This may be accompanied by
   A painted background
   Paper costume features such as hats, crowns, or masks
   Simple wood or paper props
   Fairytales, Greek mythology, or historical scenes make suitable dramatic subjects.
2. Demonstrate a skill or process, such as an experiment, art technique, handwriting, use of a computer, and so forth.
3. Plan a dramatic event such as a parade or circus.
4. Present a storytelling session, using original paintings and other artwork.

TEACHER

• Arranges for an area of the room or building where students can show others results of their independent activity. This should be a place where everyone can be a star and experience the pride of sharing creative efforts with an appreciative audience. The audience may be a small one—just a friend or two—or a large one, depending upon circumstances and interests. For formal presentations an auditorium stage can be used.

For informal sharing times, a corner with a rug and cushions suffices. Times for viewing can be scheduled or simply announced as performers are ready for the show.

Learning Area 103. Using a Dramatics Center

Subject Areas: Language Arts/Social Studies

STUDENTS

1. Act out favorite stories and poems spontaneously, unrehearsed.
2. Improvise characrter roles by dressing up in old hats, jackets, shoes, and goggles.
3. Engage in a progressive creative drama that continues over a number of sessions. The drama might be related to

Historical eras	Adventure fantasies	Running a business
Family life	Human crises	Planning a community

TEACHER

• Uses dramatic play as an opportunity for individuals to put themselves in other people's shoes and try out new roles. Often all that it takes to get started is room to do this and an assortment of clothing and simple materials for props like sheets, tarpaulins, cardboard boxes, and so on. Space can be anywhere: outdoors, in storerooms, cloakrooms, and hallways.

• Important to remember in developing dramatic play is the call for spontaneous performance. This is not a time for rehearsal or practice; "the play's the thing" here.

Learning Area 104. Using a Sound Center

Subject Areas: Music/Technology/Language Arts

STUDENTS

1. Prepare a soundtrack on a cassette player or reel-to-reel player, to accompany the showing of an original story, poem, or video program. Paintings or photographs also can be used by taping them on roll paper and then running them through an opaque projector as the soundtrack is played.
2. Use a musical record or song as inspiration for making a painting, writing a poem, or inventing a story.
3. Develop sound portraits to accompany silent films (or other films with the sound turned off). These can be tape recorded, then played as the film is shown to an audience.
4. Compose a voice-sound symphony to present as a musical show. Sounds can include buzzes, clicks, hums, whistles, grunts, moans, giggles, and so forth.

TEACHER

• Encourages children to experiment with sound effects, using their own voices and other sounds in preparing communications for an audience. In more advanced stages, the teacher explains how to edit sound material by eliminating and rearranging.

• Space for developing sound effects needs to be located where students can work without distracting others. A listening or storytelling center also can be used for enjoying informal sound productions, reserving a performance center for formal presentations.

PRODUCING MOVIES AND PLAYS
Learning Areas 105-110

The world of theater and the media arts comes alive when we produce original movies and plays as ways to communicate ideas. Students gain experience as playwrights, prop managers, layout artists, directors, and designers, in the process of shaping their ideas into story form. They also learn the discipline of selecting words and pictures carefully to make each one count. In preparing the shows, many communication skills are used:

> Arranging ideas in sequence
> Visualizing the setting of experiences
> Dealing with problems of three dimensions
> Expressing ideas through conversation rather than description
> Using oral expression for interpretation rather than reporting
> Projecting ideas, attitudes, feelings, and emotions

Different from dramatic play, which is done for its own sake, dramatic presentations require cooperative planning and an audience of some number. Productions can range from spontaneously planned ones to more formal, practiced ones; but in neither case does the teacher serve as director. While the teacher shows interest and gives guidance, the group involved develops its own plots and solves its own production problems. The scripts and stories should be the group's creations and the production a reflection of intention to communicate.

Play making demands mental discipline with words, pictures, and actions. Through writing and producing plays, individuals can learn to value these visual and verbal art forms as precise expressions of human experience. By functioning as producers, not mere receivers, they also learn the meaning of "the medium is the message."

Learning Area 105. Making Puppet Plays

Subject Areas: Language Arts/Art/Social Studies

STUDENTS

1. Find a suitable story or make one up.
2. Make a puppet for each character. These can be made from

Socks	Silhouettes
Sticks	Paper bags

> Plastic or cloth cut-outs, stuffed with soft rags or crumpled paper

3. Practice the play.
4. Find an audience who will watch it.

TEACHER

• After reading dramatic tales and poems, invites the group to act them out with stick or paper-bag puppets. Discusses various ways of making puppets, and plans with the group a puppet center where puppets can be made and puppet plays shown.

• Guides simple puppet and staging effects, when needed. A puppet stage, for example, can be either a simple box turned upside down or a stage built by the group, complete with electrical wiring, curtains, and movable scenery.

Learning Area 106. Television and Movie-Making Without Cameras

Subject Areas: Language Arts/Art/Math/Technology

STUDENTS

1. Write and illustrate original stories or redo a favorite tale in sequential pictures. These can be "rolled" out, as the story is read or taped.
2. Make an animated scene for a flipbook movie. For this, uniform sized stick figures are drawn repeatedly in strong colors on rectangular or square-shaped paper frames, also of uniform size. Drawings are stapled and pages flipped to produce an animated scene. (Or the scene can be done on adding-machine tape and rolled out quickly for the same effect.)
3. Use a computer to make an animated cartoon to show on the TV monitor screen, after learning LOGO language.

TEACHER

• Provides the basic equipment of a box with two rollers, and helps individuals to identify suitable topics, arrange ideas in proper sequence, and organize for production. Strips of paper or rolls of paper towels should be provided for pasting the pictures in sequence for "television" viewing. A movie or television center might include a TV screen, improvised with refrigerator cartons, as well as boxes and art supplies needed for preparing picture frames.

Learning Area 107. Writing and Producing Plays with Scripts

Subject Areas: Language Arts/Reading/Social Studies

STUDENTS

Work as a group to develop an original play or transpose an old tale into a modern script. In accomplishing this, they

1. Brainstorm characters, problem situations, and settings.
2. Classify, cull, and select problem situations and settings.
3. Put situations into a sequential story outline, with problems stated in Scene 1, compounded in Scene 2, and resolved in Scene 3.
4. Decide on characters and plan for two casts, to include everyone.
5. Gather dialogue, try out scenes, and select conversation.
6. Record lines in writing or on a tape recorder.
7. Decide on the play's title.
8. Select final settings and plan for special effects.
9. Set play down in script form, and duplicate copies for everyone.
10. Sign up for and hold auditions for choosing the casts.
11. Learn parts, practice play, paint scenery, and prepare scenes. (Refrigerator cartons, opened up, make four scene panels.)
12. Send out invitations to attend the play and enjoy the performance.

TEACHER

• Gives individuals and small groups responsibility for developing scripts, directing acting groups, and arranging for the presentation. Also gives guidance, as needed, but avoids taking over the management or direction of the production, which should be a culmination of the group's own efforts.

Learning Area 108. Camera-Made Movies

Subject Areas: Language Arts/Social Studies/Art/Technology

STUDENTS

Contribute to a group narrative film involving research and compilation, script writing, drawing, and sound recording. The film should be preplanned as a narrative storyboard:

1. Decide on the action.
2. Visit the scene and discuss how the shooting might go.

3. Fix the content for each shot.
4. Make pencil sketches of the shots on index cards.
5. Assemble and edit a storyboard by pinning individual frames on a long roll of paper.
6. Study the projected flow of images and story until it looks right, then number cards and use them to film the story.
7. Practice before preparing the script and doing the final shooting.

TEACHER

• In this age of electronic communication, filmmaking is a basic medium for telling stories and presenting personal interpretations of the world. Since movie-making equipment and materials can be expensive, the teacher may arrange for technical help until students acquire enough skill to develop brief film stories on their own.

Learning Area 109. Producing Radio and Television Programs

Subject Areas: Language Arts/Social Studies

STUDENTS

1. Put together a disc-jockey program, playing top musical favorites or original songs and making arrangements of various kinds.
2. Put together a news show, giving daily school and community or world news over the air. This might include interviews and commercials, as well as commentaries and reports.
3. Prepare a radio script story with sound effects.
4. Give a dramatic reading over the air, using a book, an original story or poem, an original play script, or make-believe conversations.

TEACHER

• A radio center might be anywhere recording equipment is housed; or it can be included in a dramatic play center. Here individuals improvise materials and equipment to broadcast programs and shows. They might also wish to post radio schedules, announcing shows and listening times.

• Radio scripts work well, especially for those who want to be heard but not necessarily seen in formal communication. While some radio scripts are done with improvised materials (a stick with a round metal disc becomes a quick microphone), others can be recorded on cassette or reel-to-reel recorders, or even on a local radio station (arrangements for the latter need to be made).

Learning Area 110. Videotaped Shows

Subject Areas: Language Arts/Science/Social Studies/Technology

STUDENTS

1. Make an instructional videotape for use at study centers on
   How to use video equipment   How to use cameras
   How to conduct an interview   How to make masks
2. Make camera records of classroom, lunchroom, or playground behavior to use in class discussions.
3. Make a presentation on a local TV channel or closed-circuit TV, using
   Interviews with classmates   Holiday programs or musical
   Puppet or group plays   shows
                                      Quiz shows or panel discussions
4. Prepare a simple teleplay, choosing a situation or scene, developing characters, and running it through the TV camera as an improvised product. The tape can be replayed, reviewed, and improved, as individuals wish.

TEACHER

• A half-inch, single-camera VTR system consisting of a portapak, recording deck, and playback monitor can be as simple to operate as an audiotape recorder. Sometimes the school has one, or one can be borrowed from a nearby university, resource center, or public library. A videotape can be erased and reused, keeping the running expense minimal.

• A class television studio might be set up where individuals prepare all kinds of TV communications and scripts. The camera can be mounted on a tripod, and a monitor screen (if available) can be used for viewing. As part of the planning process, the group should visit a local TV station to study the work involved in handling equipment and producing programs.

Chapter 7
Using Skills Through Self-Expression

Creative independent activities offer an unparalleled opportunity for developing the skills needed for creative living. In thinking through and carrying out their ideas, students have occasion to use all kinds of skills. Contrary to popular thinking, more skills, not fewer, become part of the daily program when the goal of creative learning takes precedence over rote learning. *Greater mastery of skills, not less, is called for in the release of creativity.*

When teachers view skills development through self-expression, they become free as never before to relate skills development to individual needs and differences. This freedom changes the role of the teacher, from the position of selecting skills to be taught, to one of teaching skills as they are identified by the learner. There is a change in attitude and purpose on the part of the teacher, and with it comes a new need to become familiar with a wide range of skills in all curriculum areas.

INDIVIDUAL DIFFERENCES IN SKILLS DEVELOPMENT

Individual differences in skills development are easily handled through creative independent activities, without undue stress on the teacher's need to plan separately for each individual. Children who have developed good study skills need not wait constantly for the teacher's directions and oversight. They can proceed on their own initiative to develop and practice the skills they need. With the skill of self-direction they can challenge themselves to learn and master new skills.

These individuals become their own teachers as they work with materials and problem solutions. When not held back for formal total class presentations and practices, which frequently are not needed, fast, alert learners can be encouraged to explore advanced arithmetic processes, composition structure, reading vocabulary, spelling techniques, and art procedures. Not only will they master skills far beyond those assigned to their so-called grade levels, but as group members they will share their learnings with others. Such sharing inspires others to look ahead and begin using skills that might be more advanced than what usually are assigned as grade-level expectations.

On the other hand, children who need longer pauses because of emotional hindrances, slower maturation, slower body rhythm, or simply more limited abilities, can take the time they need to progress. They become free from grade-level expectations that they cannot meet or meet only superficially.

Grade level expectations, arbitrarily-made plans of scope and sequence, are generally poor indicators of individual levels of skills development. A truer indicator is what students accomplish on their own. For, as they work creatively, individuals use a variety of skills and show a variety of skill needs that crisscross, even defy, grade level placements. Rather than ignore individual abilities and needs, the teacher working creatively uses them to build a personalized program of skills development.

THE TEACHER'S ROLE IN SKILLS DEVELOPMENT

Creative teachers capitalize on opportunities to teach skills on the basis of individual and group needs, not by grade-level standards. Of course, they become familiar with a range of skills found in professional books, journals, curriculum guides, and bulletins. But these are used as only one part of the grid in planning for skills development. Teachers add their own wise judgment and observations to determine which skills are needed for which children, and when.

It takes courage, after planning the environment for creative thinking and expression, for teachers to step aside long enough to observe what children can do for themselves and what they cannot do. It takes faith in the individual child's powers to learn and overcome obstacles. But teachers who develop such courage and faith also develop their ability to teach creatively.

Creative teaching does not mean sidestepping the teacher's responsibility for guiding skill growth. On the contrary, it means continually planning situations that call for students to develop new skills and practice old ones to higher levels of proficiency. This happens when the teacher makes room for both familiar and unfamiliar activities from which children can choose. Familiar activities offer security in skill practice, so children can feel comfortable with what they do. Unfamiliar activities provide a challenge to apply old skills in new ways and encourage children to reach out to learn new skills. With a wide range of possibilities presented in the daily program, individuals can find their own levels of ability and risk-taking. Hence, teachers save valuable time when they plan for functional use of skills in an environment of creative expression.

At the same time, each teacher has yet another responsibility for promoting skill development: to identify skill needs requiring direct instruction. By staying alert to the many hints for skill needs that children continually communicate as they work, the teacher finds a solid basis for teaching skills. Perhaps individuals are not using a particular skill efficiently; perhaps they are misusing certain skills for lack of understanding, or missing a skill that would propel them forward. Perhaps some children seem ready for something new in the way of skill attainment. Whatever the case, the teacher should plan to provide direct help.

Sometimes short explanations and questions do the trick. Students may catch on quickly, with insight. At other times sessions need to be planned for a skill to be introduced, practiced under close supervision, or carefully explained. These sessions are kept brief, to-the-point, and are usually handled with small groups where feedback and guidance can be given immediately. Occasionally, everyone in a class may be involved.

When stemming from activity situations, this kind of direct instruction is especially effective, for at least two reasons: one, it is presented only to those who really need it; others need not waste their time. Two, the need for it has already been experienced in context and perceived by the learners as useful to know. Students in these instances are 'ready to learn' because they have a clear purpose for learning.

PURPOSE IN SKILLS DEVELOPMENT

In the final count, there is only one thing of real importance in learning skills: ability to use the skill to achieve a purpose. With extrinsic purposes such as marks, grades, and pleasing adults, the skills themselves can become short-term affairs. But when recognized by learners as something useful—the means to creative expression—these skills take on an intrinsic purpose and become enduring.

They may read voraciously, not to read, but to get information for a collection. They may write story after story, not to write, but to get a book completed. When children work to accomplish a project, they may not be aware of the many skills they are using. If the teacher is concerned that students will go home unable to label school activity as skill work, a simple solution might be to help individuals identify the skills involved in their day's work. This can be done easily before children leave for home each day.

There are, of course, innumerable skills that can be identified and sorted into categories, ranging from communication and artistic expression to social living and scientific thinking, among others. Teachers can use skill categories not only to explain skill work to parents and other interested adults, but to plan for a well-rounded program of skills development.

COMMUNICATION SKILLS

Almost all independent activities depend on communication skills. Handwriting, spelling, composition, speaking, listening, reading, and others, being an integral part of self-expression, are easily recognized as areas for attention.

Handwriting

Handwriting activities such as those described in the sections on Writing Books, Preparing Bulletin Boards, and Organizing Collections are examples of creative production that require attention to handwriting. Whether children write only a title or label, or whether they write extensively in story and report form, preparing materials for others to read, they need to give attention to handwriting. Books go on display, exhibits travel from class to class, and bulletin boards are read by visitors. These public events provide a functional reason for practicing to improve handwriting. Printing, manuscript, and cursive handwriting skills all turn into useful skills to have when developing displays, bulletin boards, book covers, and labels, which demand a high standard for handwriting.

Because the writing is for others to read, there is a real need to use these handwriting skills:

Knowing and making all the small and capital letters
Spacing letters and words correctly
Giving attention to relative size of letters
Writing with a smooth and even quality of line
Arranging work neatly on paper
Maintaining consistent style

Selecting size of words and sentences according to headings and
  spaces
Choosing the form of writing (printing, manuscript, or cursive) to
  best fit the space and purpose

When individuals run words together and form letters so poorly that
others cannot read their writing, it makes sense to practice handwriting in
special practice periods spaced over a period of time necessary to show
improvement. During this time of practice, both the individual and the
teacher can observe progress being made as handwriting skills are ap-
plied in independent activities.

Spelling

When their own writing appears in books, on bulletin boards, on
exhibit signs, in stories for paintings, or elsewhere, children become
spelling conscious. It makes sense to spell correctly when an individual is
writing for others to read. This involves such skills as

Locating words in dictionaries by pronouncing the first few letters or
  first syllable
Sounding out words and word parts
"Seeing" words in visual recall
Recognizing words as being spelled correctly
Using phonics in building words
Using rhyming clues in spelling new words
Using prefixes and suffixes to help build words
Knowing the common sounds of beginning single consonants and
  consonant blends and the letters that represent them
Spelling words from rhyming known words
Copying with accuracy
Looking up words on charts and in dictionary files, picture dictionar-
  ies, and word dictionaries
Checking written material for spelling errors
Adding correct endings
Spelling by rote those words most commonly used in writing
Using diagraph consonant symbols
Using long and short vowel sounds and dipthongs
Changing the base when adding endings to certain words
Using compound words to make up words
Adding prefixes to known base words
Pronouncing words correctly for spelling
Writing abbreviations correctly

Spelling contractions correctly

Using hyphens correctly

Finding words in the dictionary by knowing the sequence of letters
and arrangement of words in alphabetical order

Some learners absorb many of these techniques as they write and
hunt for words; or they need only brief incidental instruction and reminders as they forge ahead in developing spelling skills. Usually these individuals are fascinated by words and want to give attention to spelling not
ordinarily covered in their grade. When the classroom environment includes materials that facilitate learning to spell words needed in composition, some children make progress in spelling skill far beyond expectations. For others, concentrating on spelling words most frequently used in
writing comes closer to meeting their need to develop with words and
word parts.

For children whose motivation for spelling is low, original writing
projects take on special significance; these students practice spelling in
context, and as they do, find more spelling words to study. Spelling, after
all, is only a way of releasing expression in written communication.
Without composition as an ongoing independent activity, no amount of
spelling practice from dictated lists will awaken a true need for correct
spelling. Furthermore, the teacher, instead of spending so much time
checking on word lists, has time to work intensively with these children in
small groups, developing their spelling power.

Composition

In creative independent activities involving writing, where individuals write for each other, for themselves, and for genuine but unknown
audiences, messages become earmarked for communication, not for grad-
ing by the teacher. As children write, they reveal their skill levels in
composition, as well as their skill needs:

Recognizing the different media of written expression and selecting
the one appropriate for the occasion (a poem, report, letter,
biography)

Expressing ideas in writing with clarity, completeness, and accuracy

Presenting ideas in an organized manner using time sequence, cause-
effect relationship, and logical relationships

Writing independently about experiences and feelings

Expressing oneself freely and spontaneously

Making words speak to intention

Expressing oneself in varied ways
Using correct verb forms
Using comparative adverb and adjective forms correctly
Using correct subject-verb agreement
Recognizing sentences
Using capital letters in names, topics, key words, and so forth
Using punctuation marks to clarify sentence meaning
Proofreading material for possible errors

Creative independent activities stress both practical and creative writing. Individuals write letters, poetry, riddles, and limericks. They write tall tales and true tales about personal experiences and make-believe incidents. They write reports, they take notes, they prepare outlines, and they keep records of their search for knowledge. They write captions for paintings, for bulletin-board displays, and for exhibits. They write instructions for playing games. They summarize information for charts and records.

In other words, individuals write because the writing is to be used. They write for purposes recognized by themselves, by their peers, by the teacher, and others. As children write down their thoughts and ideas to share with others, teachers help them to see reasons for improving their composition skills. Through this process, skill in writing over the years becomes increasingly refined.

Speaking and Listening

Getting practice in talking about what they have learned and accomplished occurs naturally through creative activities, as does listening to others talk about what they have planned and thought. As children share results of their independent efforts orally, they gain skill in reciprocal communication. They learn to express their own thoughts creatively and, in return, creatively ingest the thoughts of others as food for their own thoughts. The process is reciprocal and spiraling and calls forth a host of oral language skills:

Understanding and responding to directions
Obtaining answers to questions from what one hears
Distinguishing relevant and irrelevant material
Grasping a central idea
Discriminating between fact and opinion, fact and fantasy
Assessing resources of evidence
Contributing to group thinking

Seeking clarification of vague ideas
Realizing how speakers achieve various effects and moods
Understanding values and limitations of various communication
     media
Talking informally and easily
Choosing interesting topics of conversation
Organizing thoughts in logical sequence
Keeping to the point
Practicing social courtesies when participating in discussion
Planning presentations carefully
Giving sources of data
Pronouncing words correctly
Speaking clearly and distinctly
Extending and refining vocabulary
Using complete sentences in expressing ideas

As students speak and listen, the teacher obtains clues for directing practice needs. Sometimes these may be planned sessions where the children listen for main ideas and details, or where they learn to distinguish and evaluate facts and opinions. Certain children, mature in language, may be ready for preparing their materials in logical arrangements. Others with more limited language backgrounds may need practice in speaking fluently. In each case, plans for special sessions to provide direct help should grow from many opportunities to share orally the results of creative independent activities. Oral sharing in natural situations provides the best practice of oral language skills.

Reading

In independent activities for creative learning, reading is integrated with writing. Reading comes alive when children write books to be read by themselves and others. As they become a part of the world of books, they take a giant step toward a lifetime of reading enjoyment. Whether the book eventually finds a place in a library or goes home, it has served its purpose of deepening the purpose of reading.

Various reading skills are practiced as individuals read what they themselves or others have written:

Using meaning clues
     reading ahead to identify the word from total context
     selecting the appropriate meaning of a word to fit the context

Using word-form clues
  discriminating words of similar configuration
  using length of word and height of letters as clues
Using phonetic analysis
  pronouncing words clearly
  blending consonant and vowel sounds
Understanding words
  interpreting the meaning of prepositions
  interpreting idioms and figures of speech
Reproducing the thought of a passage
  following story sequence
  interpreting story
Reading to get detail
  restating words and sentenes in one's own language form
  following directions
Organizing ideas
  outlining information for future reference
  expressing ideas suggested through reading
Interpreting ideas
  distinguishing between narrative sentences and direct quotations
    in oral reading
  matching ideas or topics that go together

In a classroom that promotes independent activities, children not only read their homemade books and stories but they read widely in other sources to get information for reports they want to make. As they read in reference materials, they use skills such as

Understanding parts of a book, including the table of contents, index, and so on
Using periodicals
Using encyclopedias
Using dictionaries
Working from initial-letter to second- and third-letter arrangement to find words and topics while skimming the text
Locating key words in index
Glancing at sentences and paragraphs to locate words and sentences

Self-selection of reading for personal satisfaction is another independent activity that calls for reading skills practice. High-interest reading often leads to a follow-up activity involving other skills, such as writing, discussing, dramatizing, and artistic expression.

ART SKILLS

Children easily gain an array of art techniques from exploring art materials and learning to express themselves with a variety of art media used in creative independent activities. In developing their paintings; drawings; and creations in clay, textile, wood, and metal, children not only show their skill level but develop art skills such as

Seeing shape and using shading to represent fullness and contour
Decorating objects with different colors
Drawing and painting realistically
Planning clay forms by determining size, shape, and type of construction
Using many types of horizon lines
Modeling with paper over various types of construction, such as wire and wood
Experimenting with representing figures in action
Using proper tools in woodwork
Designing all-over patterns using lines and shapes
Using scissors correctly
Blending colors and experimenting with the use of vivid color
Measuring to achieve accurate results
Seeing possibilities of color blends and shades
Handling various sizes of easel brushes
Representing near and far shapes with accuracy
Cutting and sewing materials
Realizing how main ideas can be expressed through dominant figure or color groups in a picture
Working with three-dimensional paper

Skill needs often become obvious as individuals work with varied media. In determining what guidance to provide, teachers might ask themselves questions such as

What experiences has the student had with this medium?
Where does the child fumble when working in a free, unstructured situation?
How well does this pupil make a particular kind of object?
Could the individual handle the next step of skill difficulty?

In answering these questions on an individual basis, teachers make certain that creative activities and skill growth in artistic expression go hand in hand as part of the daily program.

SKILLS OF SOCIAL LIVING AND INTERPERSONAL RELATIONS

Along with skills in communication and artistic expression, it is important to teach the vital skills associated with interpersonal relationships, such as living harmoniously and productively with others. For example, when a group of children takes responsibility for arranging a display, members learn to share. Preparing a bulletin board as a small group's project calls for mutual planning. Constructing a puppet stage invites cooperative effort. Making daily and weekly plans together requires listening to the opinions of others.

During times like these, whether individuals work with a partner, small group, or large group, many skills are involved in group procedures.

Giving suggestions for the group to consider
Deciding when proposals sound most promising
Considering the kinds of records needed for guides
Presenting alternatives clearly to all
Deciding when to delegate tasks to a committee
Selecting activities most central to the agreed-upon plan
Determining assignments of committees
Choosing people best qualified for a particular job
Considering materials needed
Exploring sources of needed materials
Apportioning time for the job
Deciding how to share results of committee work
Deciding what to do when a plan fails
Reporting progress and needs during planning and evaluation
    periods
Judging the success of work on the basis of goals set up
Analyzing satisfactions gained from the work
Explaining reasons for disagreements
Using courteous language and gestures
Standing by agreements
Sharing materials
Seeking to understand the causes of others' behavior
Appraising personal strengths and limitations
Accepting contributions of all members
Coping with frustration and strain in socially acceptable ways
Resolving conflicting values

These skills of social living need more than cursory attention to be mastered. Sometimes everyone in a group may need direct instruction in ways to speak courteously, disagree intelligently, serve as a group leader, or resolve conflicts. At other times, teachers will give direct guidance to individuals who need special help in learning how to contribute to a common cause, give and take to solve common problems, share with others, and so on. In an environment which supports frequent peer collaboration, the development of skills for interpersonal relations need not be left to chance.

SKILLS OF REFERENCE STUDY AND SCIENTIFIC AND MATHEMATICAL REASONING

In both group and individual work, children apply a variety of reference study skills and skills of scientific-mathematical reasoning. As they search for information, explore self-service areas for materials to implement ideas and answer questions, or solve problems related to creative production, they use skills like

Deriving principles and generalizations
Applying information and generalizations in new situations
Evaluating adequacy of solutions
Selecting information pertinent to problem solution
Using illustrative materials to convey ideas
Seeing relationships among data
Preparing data in graphic or pictorial form
Preparing summaries and outlines
Organizing material from notes
Interviewing to obtain information
Observing during demonstrations
Keeping records of observations
Using maps, globes, and atlases
Using map and globe scales of distances
Locating physical and cultural features
Interpreting map symbols to obtain information
Counting objects by different groupings
Reading and writing number symbols
Recording facts of adding, subtracting, dividing, and multiplying
Comparing sizes and shapes
Using various measurements to obtain height, weight, content, and
    capacity
Recognizing money denominations
Telling time
Finding parts of one object, or of various groupings
Sensing the essential elements of the problem within the total
    situation

"Guessing" intelligently
Using a variety of approaches in defining a problem
Advancing possible explanations
Working through a hypothesis to the testing stage
Finding causes for everyday occurrences

Students, working independently for creative purposes, confront these skill needs directly as they work to solve problems and accomplish their goals. When children map out a family trip, for example, they face the need to show distances; with a friend or two, or with the teacher's help, they may practice drawing map scales before preparing one for their map. Likewise, when children create story-problems using numbers to illustrate the use of multiplication and division of fractions, they may need to practice multiplying and dividing in order to prepare accurate answer sheets.

Children who keep weekly records of the weather or temperature use calendar skills, time-telling skills, and scientific observation skills. Those who make a geography-literature anthology use globes and maps to locate places and get proper spellings; they number and sort anthology pages, plan a table of contents, an index, or a glossary; they use atlases and almanacs to get information on matters of interest, and organize notes in preparation for reporting. In short, involvement in a range of open-ended, independent activities assures both the development and practice of many reference skills using mathematical and scientific thinking.

SKILLS AND CREATIVE LEARNING: SOME LAST WORDS

There are many skills and skill categories other than those listed, which function as part of independent activities for creative learning. There are musical skills—composing tunes, making musical notations, developing rhythms, and the like; there are movement skills, dramatic skills, construction skills. The range of skills covered is virtually limitless when the curriculum includes a wide range of activities.

Teachers who value creativity sufficiently to plan for integrated skill development do not cover skills so much as they *uncover* individual abilities and needs, and teach accordingly. There is no reason to conclude that skills are being neglected just because the teacher no longer spends most of the day presenting formal lessons to a large group. On the contrary, by staying alert to which skills individuals are learning easily on their own and which ones need boosting or guidance, and for whom, the teacher shifts dramatically from formal lesson teaching to intensive, individualized and personalized work with children. By observing which skills seem urgent for which children, and juxtaposing observations with a teacher-made list of priorities, the teacher makes curriculum decisions: what skills should be emphasized for whom, and how.

In an environment with ample opportunity for both individualized study and independent activities in searching, organizing, originating, and communicating, skills will be developed both directly and indirectly. The 3-R skills get their due, but should be kept in balance with other skills needed for students to survive and thrive in today's world. In this era of skills bombardment and knowledge explosion, it seems imperative for us to reexamine and reprioritize our expectations for children's skill learning. By making sure that a broad scope of skills development exists, we also make sure that balance is maintained; demands for new skills are easily accommodated and integrated into the daily school program. More importantly, with balance, the multiple facets of intelligence are fully recognized and cherished, as they should be. Personal intelligence and bodily-kinesthetic intelligence are valued as highly as linguistic or logico-mathematical intelligence; musical intelligence wins as much respect as spatial intelligence. In this framework, all children—whatever their particular forms of intelligence—find equal opportunities for fulfillment. This is the way of a democratic society. Everyone counts, and counts equally. In a school designed to promote democracy, every student has the right to not only be accepted, but to be enthusiastically guided toward fulfillment—both as an individual and as a group member.

The creative teacher courageously accepts the democratic vision of fulfillment as a basic goal for classroom life. This goal entails enabling children to celebrate their uniqueness as individuals while still embracing their commonalities with all people. Teacher guidance, in this view, becomes a matter of helping each child contribute responsibly to cooperative, group endeavors, while reaching out freely toward individuation. Would we want otherwise, in a shrinking world and an expanding universe? As the author Bernard Malamud wrote in his novel, *The Fixer*: "The purpose of having freedom for ourselves is to create it for others."

SELECTED
BIBLIOGRAPHY

INDEX

Selected Bibliography

GENERAL

Cohen, Dorothy. *The Learning Child*. New York: Pantheon, 1972.

Drew, Walter, ed. *Motivating Today's Students*. Palo Alto, CA: Education Today, 1974.

Gross, Beatrice, and Gross, Ronald, eds. *Will I Grow in the Classroom?* New York: Delta, 1974.

Holt, John. *What Do I Do Monday?* New York: E. P. Dutton, 1970.

Howe, Leland, and Howe, Mary. *Personalizing Education*. New York: Hart, 1975.

Howes, Virgil. *Informal Teaching in the Open Classroom*. New York: Macmillan, 1974.

Kohl, Herbert. *On Teaching*. New York: Bantam, 1977.

Kohl, Herbert. *Basic Skills*. New York: Bantam, 1984.

Moorman, Chuck, and Dishon, Dee. *Our Classroom: We Can Learn Together*. Englewood Cliffs, NJ: Prentice-Hall, 1983.

Mossman, Lois. *The Activity Concept*. New York: Macmillan, 1938.

Samples, Bob, Charles, Cheryl, and Barnhart, Dick. *The Whole School Book*. Menlo Park, CA, 1977.

READING AND WRITING

Allen, R. Van. *Language Experiences in Communication*. Boston: Houghton Mifflin, 1976.

Ashton-Warner, Sylvia. *Spinster: The Story of a Teacher of Maori Children*. New York: Simon and Schuster, 1958.

Ashton-Warner, Sylvia. *Teacher*. New York: Simon and Schuster, 1963.

Graves, Donald. *Writing: Teacher and Children at Work*. Exeter, NH: Heinemann, 1983.

Holdaway, Don. *The Foundations of Literacy*. New York: Ashton Scholastic, 1979.

Povey, Gail, and Fryer, Jeanne. *Personalized Reading*. Los Angeles: International Center for Educational Development, 1977.

Smith, Frank. *Reading Without Nonsense*, 2d ed. New York: Teachers College Press, 1985

Veatch, Jeannette. *Reading in the Elementary School*. New York: Richard Owen, 1984.

Veatch, Jeannette, et al. *Key Words to Reading*. Columbus, OH: Charles Merrill, 1979.

WORKING WITH COMPUTERS

Lipscomb, Susan, and Zuanich, Margaret. *Basic Fun: Computer Games, Puzzles and Problems Children Can Write*. New York: Avon, 1982.

Malone, Linda, and Johnson, Jerry. *Basic Discoveries—A Problem-Solving Approach to Beginning Programming*. Oak Lawn, IL: Creative Publications, 1983.

Moore, Margaret. *Logo Discoveries*. Oak Lawn, IL: Creative Publications, 1984.

WORKING WITH MEDIA

Crossword Magic: Disk for Apple II Computer. Oak Lawn, IL: Creative Publications.

Laybourne, Kit, and Cianciolo, Pauline, eds. *Doing the Media*. New York: McGraw-Hill, 1978.

Rice, Susan, and Mukerji, Rose, eds. *Children are Centers for Understanding Media*. Washington, DC: Association for Childbased Education International, 1973.

LEARNING CENTERS

Allen, R. Van, and Allen, Clarice. *Language Experience Adventures*. Boston: Houghton Mifflin, 1982.

ACEI. *Learning Centers: Children on Their Own*. Washington, DC: Association for Childbased Education International, 1970.

Kahl, David, and Gast, Barbara. *Learning Centers in the Open Classroom*. Los Angeles: International Center for Educational Development, 1974.

Loughlin, Catherine, and Suina, Joseph. *The Learning Environment: An Instructional Strategy*. New York: Teachers College Press, 1982.

Rogovin, Anne. *Let Me Do It*. New York: Thomas Crowell, 1980.

ART, MUSIC, AND DRAMA

Hurwitz, Al. *Programs of Promise: Art in the Schools.* New York: Harcourt Brace Jovanovich, 1972.

Langstaff, Nancy and Sproul, Adelaide, eds. *Exploring with Clay.* Washington, DC: Association for Childhood Educational International, 1979.

List, Lynne. *Music, Art and Drama Experiences for the Elementary Curriculum.* New York: Teachers College Press, 1982.

Ramsey, Marjorie, ed. *It's Music.* Washington, DC: Association for Childhood Education International, 1984.

Romney, Emily. *Musical Instrument Recipe Book: Elementary Science Study.* New York: McGraw-Hill, 1971.

Sheehy, Emma. *Children Discover Music and Dance.* New York: Teachers College Press, 1968.

Smith, Nancy. *Experience and Art: Teaching Children to Paint.* New York: Teachers College Press, 1983

SOCIAL STUDIES AND SCIENCE

Ahern, John, and Lucas, Nanci. *Ideas: A Handbook for Elementary Social Studies.* New York: Harper & Row, 1070

Barth, Beth. *Teacher's Guide for Mapping: Elementary Science Study.* New York: McGraw-Hill, 1971.

Darrow, Helen. *Social Studies for Understanding.* New York: Teachers College Press, 1963.

Johnson, David, and Johnson, Roger. *Learning Together and Alone: Cooperation, Competition and Individualization.* Englewood Cliffs, NJ: Prentice-Hall, 1975.

Mugge, Dorothy, ed. *Involvement Bulletin Boards.* Washington, DC: Association for Childhood Education International, 1970.

Roche, Ruth. *The Child and Science.* Washington, DC: Association for Childhood Education International, 1977.

Schmidt, Victor, and Rockcastle, Verne. *Teaching Science with Everyday Things.* New York: McGraw-Hill, 1982.

Wurman, Richard, ed. *Yellow Pages of Learning Resources.* Cambridge, MA: MIT Press, 1972.

WORKING WITH SELF-CONCEPT

Canfield, Jack, and Wells, Harold. *100 Ways to Enhance Self-Concept in the Classroom.* Englewood Cliffs, NJ: Prentice-Hall, 1976.

Hendricks, Gay. *The Centering Book: Awareness Activities for Children, Parents and Teachers*. Englewood Cliffs, NJ: Prentice-Hall, 1975.

Purkey, William. *Inviting School Success: A Self-Concept Approach to Teaching and Learning*. Belmont, CA: Wadsworth, 1978.

THEORETICAL BACKGROUND

Archambault, Reginald, ed. *John Dewey on Education: Selected Writings*. Chicago: University of Chicago Press, 1964.

Elkind, David. *Child Development and Education: A Piagetian Perspective*. New York: Oxford University Press, 1976.

Ferguson, Marilyn. *The Aquarian Conspiracy*. Los Angeles: Tarcher, 1980.

Freire, Paulo. *Pedagogy of the Oppressed*. New York: Seabury Press, 1970.

Gallagher, Jeannette, and Reid, D. *The Learning Theory of Piaget and Inhelder*. Monterey, CA: Brooks, Cole, 1981.

Gardner, Howard. *Frames of Mind: The Theory of Multiple Intelligences*. New York: Basic Books, 1985.

May, Rollo. *The Courage to Create*. New York: Norton, 1975.

Pearce, Joseph. *The Magical Child*. New York: Dalton, 1977.

Rogers, Carl. *Freedom to Learn for the 80's*. Columbus, OH: Charles Merrill, 1984.

Index

Subject Areas are listed as **bold** entries.